East Anglia by Rail

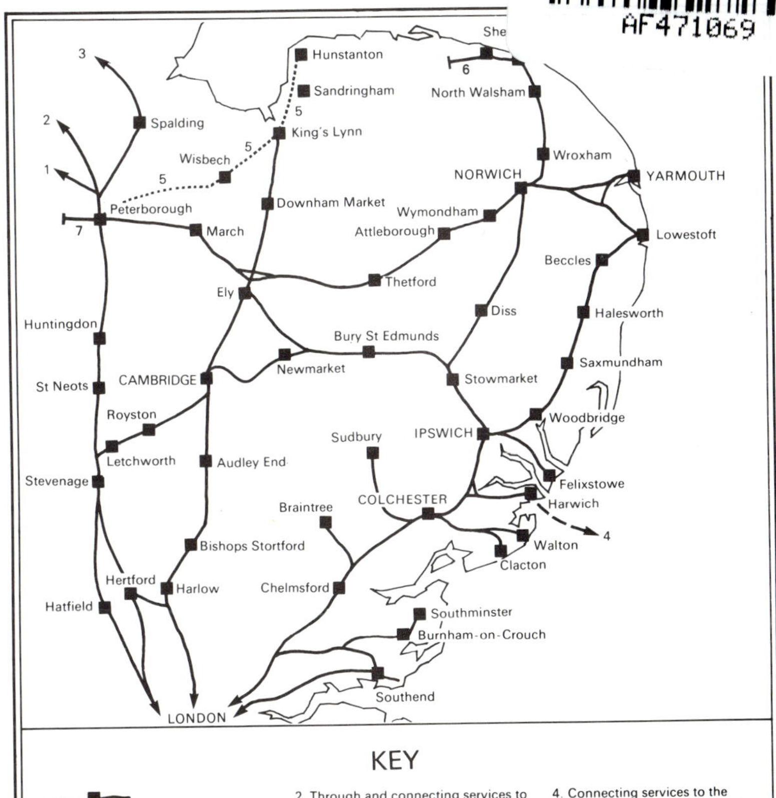

A guide to the routes, scenery and towns

FOREWORD

by the Chairman of the East Anglian Branch, Railway Development Society

Welcome to East Anglia! Thank you for buying this book, which I hope will make your travels more enjoyable.

Last year, our Society published the first edition of *East Anglia by Rail*, which raised a tremendous amount of interest, and has encouraged us to compile this second, enlarged edition. I should like to take this opportunity of thanking all those who have made the publication possible. As before, any profits which we make from sales of the book will assist us in our campaign for even better rail services in East Anglia.

Since the last edition, little has changed in East Anglia's places of interest. Our lovely beaches, country inns, first-class fishing, delightful cricket grounds are all still there, awaiting the visitor. All the East Anglian towns and villages go on, as they have done through the ages, showing a charm unmatched anywhere else in England.

There have been considerable changes on the railway scene since the first edition. The long-awaited modernisation of the East Suffolk line is now well under way. Modern open crossings and radio signalling are being installed and work should be completed by the end of 1985. If this is the success that we all think it will be, then we hope the idea will be extended elsewhere on the secondary lines. You can rest assured that the primroses along the route have not been disturbed by all the work!

The Government has approved, at long last, plans to electrify the East Coast Main Line from King's Cross to Edinburgh, along the western side of our region. The Railway Development Society has campaigned for this project for many years. Once completed, it is likely to bring substantial improvements in reliability and punctuality, though probably only a modest improvement in speed.

Electrification between Colchester and Norwich is proceeding well and work has started on electrifying the Bishop's Stortford–Cambridge line. This naturally means that railway history and items of railway engineering of the past are fast disappearing. Level crossings are being automated, manual signal-boxes being dismantled, bridges being heightened. Yet remnants of the old Great Eastern Railway can still be seen in places – the ironwork on pillars and seats at Thetford Station is an excellent example.

The Railway Development Society, as an independent, voluntary body for rail-users, will continue to promote the local rail network, supported by its corporate members, the local Line Users' Associations. Every paytrain service in our region has a Users' Association, playing an active part in its promotion. We are grateful for their vigilance and support.

Haverhill, Long Melford, Aldeburgh, Saffron Walden, and Hunstanton have no rail services; but there are campaigns to have passenger services restored on a limited basis, to serve St Ives, Wisbech, and Dereham. The 1981 Amendment to the Transport Act of 1962 (promoted by Tony Speller, MP) could well be used to secure at least experimental passenger services for these three growing towns and their not inconsiderable catchment areas.

I remain convinced that East Anglia is very much underrated. There are things to do and see which cater for every interest – and I do not say this just because I come from East Anglian stock of many generations. Boadicea has been dead for a very long time, we do not cover ourselves with woad these days and, while our regional dialects may be confusing at first – a welcome awaits you. Hoping that your stay in East Anglia will be a pleasant one – safe journeys!

52 Manor Park
Histon
Cambridge

Steve Wilkinson
March 1985

CONTENTS

KEY TO LINE DIAGRAMS

ELY Staffed station; booking-office; train information available; seats and shelter at station.

Beccles Unstaffed station: pay on the train.

WISBECH Served by British Rail bus service.

WANSFORD Preserved station. Open only on certain days; facilities not necessarily available at other times.

Continuous line: no intermediate stations between those shown.

Norwich Through trains from the line shown on the diagram to the destination named.

Broken line: intermediate stations not shown.

L — Ladies' toilet.

G — Gents' toilet.

①t — Train information board at station.

①tb — Train and bus information boards at station.

T-FB — Travellers-Fare Buffet.

B — Buffet.

Bks(Dks M-S am) — Bookstall (here shown serving take-away drinks Monday to Saturday mornings. Other letters M, F, S, are combined as required).

S — Seats.

Sr — Shelter (waiting-room, or awning, or bus-stop type).

ILFORD Station facilities not shown.

Taxi – Taxi rank at station, or local taxi firm has office at station. L.St. – London (Liverpool Street). K.X. – London (King's Cross). B'ham – Birmingham.

INTRODUCTION

There can be few more relaxing or instructive ways of visiting a region of Britain than by train. Furthermore, if the region is East Anglia, then the varied scenery, the extensive waterways, and the gently undulating routes will make that pilgrimage so much more exciting, for the counties of Hertfordshire and Essex, Norfolk, Suffolk, and Cambridgeshire are too large for a comprehensive survey by car; and their cross-country roads often too narrow and congested to make motoring much of a pleasure. To prove the point of this, try leaving Ipswich by train or by car on any weekday at about 6.30 pm and see who arrives within two hours at Peterborough the more enlightened and refreshed.

The railway network of East Anglia, a mere shadow of its pre-war splendour, is yet more generously endowed with routes than, for example, the scenic west side of Cumbria, Cornwall, or Wales. From west to east or south to north, by suburban electric or diesel railcar – sometimes even by Inter-City express – you will learn much of the architecture, the people of the area, and their life-styles. Above all, you will see the farming year in all its varied moods and scenes; the Broads in summer, or a winter sunset in the Fens, leave an indelible impression on the mind of the enthusiastic visitor.

East Anglia by Rail will take you on fifteen journeys of surprise from London in the south to Lowestoft in the east, Sheringham in the north and as far west as Peterborough. If you have the time, stop at some of the cities and market towns mentioned. Sample the East Anglian way of life at first hand with local dishes like Fenland pie in Whittlesey, or local beer at, well, almost every station. Each rail journey has been written with the visitor in mind who has no car. Consequently, the stops and diversions are restricted to places within walking distance of the station, though the possibilities of short cycle and bus trips from railheads are also given.

If you take your travels very seriously, then there are numerous local guidebooks that can be purchased or borrowed to fill in the information that we have been obliged to trim. For example, almost every church you visit will have its own expertly written and highly detailed leaflet to guide you.

Finally, don't be put off by the estimated cost of your journeys. Within a generously prescribed area, the Anglia Ranger One-Day and Seven-Day ticket will give you almost unlimited travel around East Anglia, with any number of breaks of journey permitted, for most of the year. It is not possible to travel in and out of London with one, but you can get within striking distance of the suburbs. Ranger tickets are extraordinarily good value for money (one of the contributors to this book set a record by travelling $676\frac{1}{4}$ miles in twenty-four hours with one!) and can be purchased at all staffed stations and travel centres, from British Rail Agents and, in the case of the One-Day Ranger, from the guard on the train.

LIVERPOOL STREET–NORWICH

by Steve Hewitt

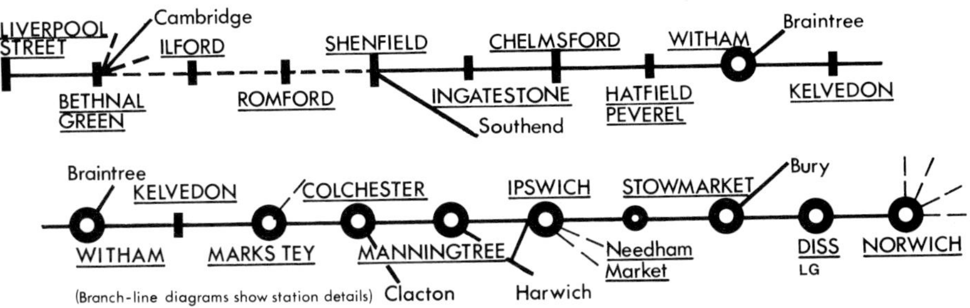

A journey from London to East Anglia starts from one of the capital's biggest and busiest termini – Liverpool Street. Built in 1874–75 to replace the former terminus known as Shoreditch, Liverpool Street is the gateway to East Anglia. Trains leave here at regular intervals to Clacton, Southend, Cambridge, and to our destination – Norwich.

On leaving Liverpool Street the train takes a very slow course crossing the network of lines that merge from the nineteen platforms, serving 160,000 passengers daily, into just six lines. The train ascends to Bethnal Green Junction, then gathers speed for its 115-mile run to Norwich.

For the first half-hour one can appreciate the actual size of the great metropolis, passing through a large number of townships, such as Stratford (where the Great Eastern Railway built its locomotives), Ilford, and Shenfield. Over the years, these townships became interlinked with their rows of terraced houses and modern tower blocks, then suburban semis, all helping to provide the workforce for London's industry and commerce. They are served by a regular interval service of electric multiple units, allowing the Inter-City trains a swift and uninterrupted run.

The first major town reached is Chelmsford. Many Norwich-bound trains do not stop here, but some do and help convey commuters back and forth to the capital. Chelmsford has a fairly extensive industrial area and to the left can be seen the premises of Marconi, the electronics firm and the town's largest employer. To the right is the cathedral and shopping centre.

Leaving Chelmsford behind, we continue our run, often close to the dual-carriageway A12, where the train can race the road traffic. Indeed, along this section of line, speeds can touch 100 mph as we flash through expanded commuter towns like Witham and Kelvedon, and soon we see Colchester on its hill to the right.

Colchester is a town which has grown steadily since the arrival of the railway in 1843 and is the first main stop for most of the Norwich-bound trains. Here you can change trains to visit the seaside at Clacton or for a visit to the charming Stour Valley town of Sudbury.

For two decades, the overhead electric wires stopped just beyond Colchester. In December 1981, British Rail finally secured Government approval to extend them to Norwich, and under the Anglian Electrification Scheme they are destined to reach Norwich in 1987. Our train presses on to Manningtree, giving us a grandstand view of the Stour Valley, immortalised by the eighteenth-century

London–Norwich Inter-City train speeds through the Essex countryside. In May 1985, electric locomotives took over from diesels on this section. (*Photo:* J. A. Howie)

artist, John Constable. Manningtree is well known as the junction for Harwich and the Continent. It is less well known that a mere mile or so from the station, across water-meadows, is Flatford Mill, a beauty-spot in the heart of Constable country.

We pass into Suffolk, climb through the deep Brantham Cutting and through hilly country before descending Belstead Bank, approaching Ipswich. On the right, one can see the new Orwell Bridge, part of the Ipswich By-pass scheme. The town's original station was beside the River Orwell until a short tunnel – the only one on this line – was built under Stoke Hill. It is believed to be the first curved tunnel to be built in this country.

All trains call at Ipswich Station, serving the business and commercial centre of Suffolk. Here you can change trains for Felixstowe and the East Suffolk line, whose junction lies just beyond the goods yard. In the build-up to the arrival of electrification at Ipswich, which is due in May 1985, a lot of work such as stone-cleaning and repointing has been done to enhance the appearance of this fine old station. British Rail aim to bring down the journey time from London to Ipswich to just one hour by the fastest train when the electric service commences. Norwich-bound trains will change locomotives here until the whole scheme is complete in

1987. Ipswich is also to be the terminus of a semi-fast electric multiple unit service from London, thus giving it three trains every two hours, on average, to and from the capital.

Leaving Ipswich behind we now commence the final leg of our journey, through some lovely Suffolk countryside. The scenery is mainly rural as we speed along the Gipping Valley and then across flat arable farmland, broken only by the odd cluster of houses whose only remaining link with the railway is a wayside halt now overgrown and disused. Most of these wayside stations were closed in 1966, but in some of the villages there has, in recent years, been pressure to re-open them. However, we do pass through two quite large communities, the first of which, Stowmarket, is served not only by an increasing number of Inter-City trains, but also by Ipswich–Cambridge services. The station at Stowmarket – a listed building – has recently been refurbished, the platforms lengthened considerably, better facilities for the disabled installed, and the exterior cleared. A few minutes' walk from the station lies the Museum of East Anglian Life, the only open-air museum in East Anglia. Re-erected buildings and restored agricultural machinery, craft demonstrations and special events – all illustrate East Anglian life through the centuries.

Leaving Stowmarket behind, we pass Haughley Junction, though all that remains of its station is a signal-cabin. Here trains to Cambridge and Peterborough diverge cross-country. Until July 1952 it was also the terminus of the Mid-Suffolk Light Railway from Laxfield. This line was used a great deal, especially during wartime, as a supply line to airfields at Mendlesham and Horham.

Our train speeds on past the endless rows of overhead cable poles, marching like some invading army relentlessly on to Norwich. We pass through the village of Mellis, until 1964 the junction for a short branch line to Eye, and on to the town of Diss, crossing the infant River Waveney as we go.

Diss is a thriving little community, whose station, with its recently lengthened platforms and new footbridge, serves as a railhead for a wide area of North Suffolk and South Norfolk. The town centre, to the west of the station, is given added character by its unusual Mere. Diss was also the junction for one of the few 'estate' railways – the Scole Railway – built in 1850 by local landowner, William Betts, who saw it as an ideal opportunity to send his market-garden produce quicker to London. After Betts's death, however, the line fell into disrepair and was lifted in 1886.

North of Diss we speed across more arable land, through the village of Burston (scene of the famous school strike in the early twentieth century), past Tivetshall (junction of the Waveney Valley Railway to Beccles via Bungay and closed to passengers in January 1953), and past Forncett junction to a branch line to Wymondham on the Breckland line opened in 1881 to allow the Great Eastern Railway better access to North Norfolk and its then growing seaside resorts, thus avoiding Norwich. The growth of travel never materialised and apart from being a vital link during the floods of 1912, when the line to the north of Norwich was blocked, it soon fell into disuse and closed to passengers in 1939.

Very soon we approach Norwich with views of the pleasant Tas Valley to the right and the Tacolneston television transmitter to the left. Just before reaching Norwich, you can judge how big the city has grown, with endless rows of housing broken up only by the site of the new cattle market. We pass over a five-arch viaduct, with the River Yare and Breckland line below, swing to the right, down into the valley across Trowse Swing Bridge (due for renewal by 1988) and past Crown Point Locomotive and Carriage Depot (opened in 1982). Your journey ends in six-platform Norwich Thorpe, sole survivor of the city's three former termini.

LIVERPOOL STREET–ELY

by Peter Wakefield

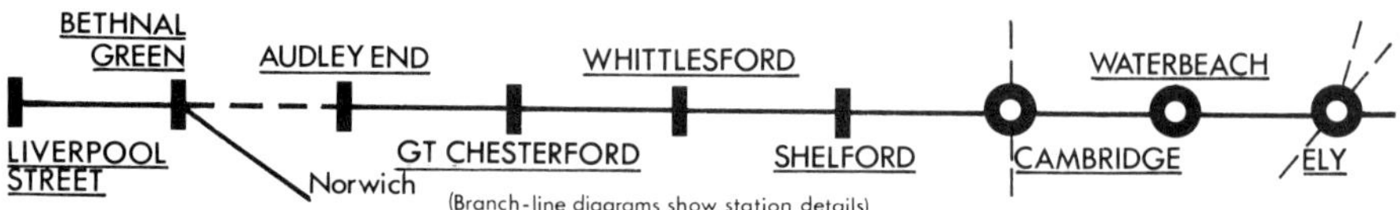

Fenland trains traditionally leave London from Liverpool Street Station – a gloomy cavernous edifice to be got out of as quickly as possible for some, but to many generations of East Anglians, a friendly outpost of home. Trains to the west of the region generally take the Bethnal Green–Hackney Downs–Lea Valley route. However, in passing, it should be noted that three other routes are available – used in emergencies at differing frequencies:

1   Bethnal Green–Stratford–Temple Mills–Lea Valley.
2   Bethnal Green–Hackney Downs–Edmonton–Cheshunt.
3   Bethnal Green–Stratford–North London line–Finsbury Park and thence via the Great Northern route through Hitchin and Royston to Cambridge.

The second of these routes is probably the most frequently used diversion. Trains for the Fens leave from Platform 7 as a rule. It is a slow roar as the diesel locomotive gets a grip of the train up the bank to Bethnal Green. Just as the locomotive 'gets going', it has to make a rapid brake application to take the route that veers sharply to the left from the Colchester line. Again it roars – after the curve and junction are negotiated and the train snakes along the roof-top-high viaduct to Hackney Downs Station, a grimy, decaying area of the city. Just beyond Hackney Downs, the train bears to the right over another junction and then underground through a series of tunnels under Clapton.

A few minutes more and we experience another rapid slowing. This time, the train turns sharply to the left, passing over yet another junction. The restrained speed is maintained for half a mile or so, the locomotive easily visible on the 'near side' as it leads its train round and down a long curve to join the line from Temple Mills to the north via Cambridge. After joining this line, the train heads up towards the headwaters of the River Lea – its valley in the area of Tottenham being wide and, until recently, marshy. The train rapidly gathers speed, passing many suburban stations that serve the thousands of new houses which have sprouted all along the line.

In the Cheshunt/Waltham Cross area, evidence is seen of the horticulture that brought its original prosperity, in the form of many glasshouses. At Cheshunt, the line from Hackney Downs via Edmonton trails in. Just over three miles on, the train speeds through the important passenger and freight station of Broxbourne, which is also the junction for Hertford.

The fastest trains continue on through Harlow Town, some twenty-two miles and twenty-six minutes from London, to the slowing necessary to take the curves through Bishop's Stortford (thirty and a quarter miles). (Many expresses, though, stop at both Harlow – one of the first post-war New Towns – and Bishop's Stortford.)

After Bishop's Stortford, it seems as if London is finally left behind. The train steadily climbs through the rolling chalk country of north-west Essex to the summit of the line at Elsenham. (Elsenham is one of the six village stations between

Bishop's Stortford and Cambridge that have their separate local service and still look very much as they did when they were built.)

Once through Elsenham, the line twists and turns in a most surprising way for a main line in lowland England. The actual railway is very well engineered and high speeds are always obtained on this very smooth section. Just after passing the picturesque village of Newport, some expresses start to slow for the busy railhead station of Audley End. The large and always full car park testifies to its popularity.

The locomotive faces another pull up out of Audley End. Its noise is accentuated by the roar that develops as it pulls through the two Audley End tunnels. Speed is again resumed and the express gallops through the remaining three stations and fourteen miles to Cambridge.

Between Great Chesterford and Whittlesford stations is the large CIBA-Geigy chemical works, two or three fields away from the line to the west. It was connected to the main railway in 1980 and a large siding complex built, with the aid of a grant under Section 8 of the 1974 Railways Act. This enables many thousands of tons of raw materials and finished products to keep on the rails and off our overcrowded and polluted highways – an immense benefit to us all.

All trains stop at Cambridge – a busy passenger and freight junction. Several million people use its extremely long single through platform each year, many of them tourists from all over the world, visiting the many attractions the city offers. Others change trains for Newmarket, Bury St Edmunds, Royston, March, or Peterborough.

However, every two hours, the fastest trains from London continue northwards and out on to the Fens. These are reached in the northern suburbs of the city as the train gathers speed to cross the River Cam at Chesterton Junction. Here the St Ives freight branch veers away to the north-west, with the vast British Rail track engineering works built into the 'fork' of the two rail lines. The express only passes through one station – Waterbeach – in the fifteen miles to Ely, demonstrating the low population density of this area. Its fertile soils, however, feed more of our population than any other equivalent region.

Sixteen minutes after leaving Cambridge, the express again slows to a stop at the very busy rail centre of Ely. The station here is in the valley of the River Ouse, which is just to the east. The city lies on a hill to the west, clustered round the massive and beautiful cathedral. Trains connect here with all parts of East Anglia – this station has services to/from Ipswich, Bury St Edmunds, Peterborough, Thetford, Norwich, Great Yarmouth, and King's Lynn. Many freight trains pass through Ely's complicated junction, some of whose wagons bear the initials of owning companies in places as far apart as Czechoslovakia, Hungary, West Germany, Italy, France, and Spain. These come on the fast freight trains that run to the north of Britain from the ferry terminal at Harwich, all passing through Ely – this Crewe of the East!

PETERBOROUGH–ELY

by Ian Brakewell

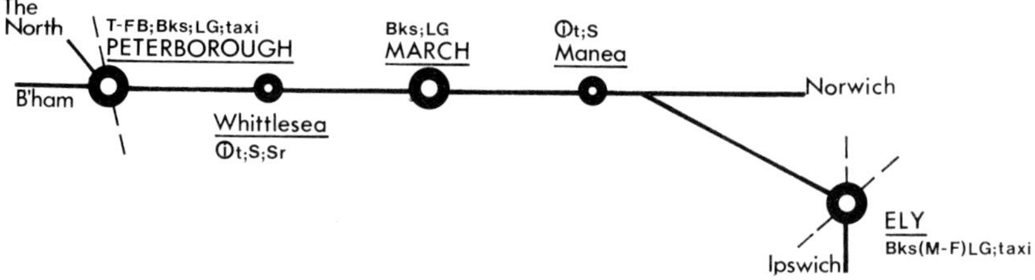

The East Coast Main Line, taking as it does express trains between London and Scotland, could be described as the western boundary of East Anglia. And it is at a point along this line that the visitor must, if travelling farther east, decide to alight. There can be no better place for him to do this than the thriving, bustling development city of Peterborough, where High Speed Trains provide a service to the capital – now only forty-seven minutes away. Here the station and its associated buildings are all modern, redesigned and rebuilt in the 1970s. The city, too, glows with consumer prosperity as shopping centres, pedestrian precincts, and a magnificent cathedral welcome visitors from far afield. The benefits of Development Corporation grants have enabled Peterborough to boast facilities among the best in England. Arts and leisure entertainments abound; and for the railway buff there's even a steam railway that chugs westward to Wansford along the valley of the River Nene.

But other delights lie ahead for the unsuspecting traveller. The train connections for East Anglia depart, surprisingly, from the western side of Peterborough Station. West to east locomotive-hauled trains jostle for space with Spalding and Ely diesel multiple units on Platform 5. The reasons for this are probably lost in the mists of operational antiquity, but no difficulty is encountered today. Our slower-moving eastbound train simply drops below the level of the old Great Northern main line, and then, without a by-your-leave, smartly passes beneath it, curving sharply away to the east as it does so. And here we are in a diesel railcar or following the throaty roar of a Norwich-bound express actually passing through the 'gateway' to East Anglia. We move smartly beyond the site of the old station at Peterborough East and travel in a direction that, as the crow flies, is indeed due east.

What sights lie ahead, what an expanse of unending flatness is to meet the eye as for mile after mile we will see the horizon and the land beyond it! Cambridgeshire is the county that will make eyes ache and hill-lovers forever despair of seeing rising ground again. Now, as if to emphasise the fact that we are in a new world, the brick-pits of King's Dyke gape around us like moon craters. Gaunt chimneys and brick stacks announce our imminent arrival at Whittlesey, first stopping-off place in the Fens.

At Whittlesey, a delightful town with a butter cross, manor house, and the Church of St Andrew to visit, we witness the first example of railway legend being at variance with local practice. Quite alone now in the district, British Rail still persists in its spelling of the name as 'Whittlesea'. Here we might pause for a while to remark on the number of places yet to come whose name ends in 'ea' or 'ey'. Throughout the Fens, this suffix reminds the visitor of the island nature of the

Peterborough–Cambridge DMU crosses the flooded 'Wash' of the Bedford Levels. (*Photo:* John C. Baker)

region before proper drainage was to produce the landscape we have today. In Old English, 'ealan' or 'iegland' signified island, and it is said that through appropriate derivation slight rises in the swampy flooded ground were thus suffixed, as Thorney, Eastrea, Ely (Eel Island). In times of mist and heavy rain and with treacherous water currents, where a king might lose all of his treasures at the turn of the tide, such island homes would have been welcome refuges.

As we continue our journey through wheat fields, beet fields, or barley fields, where the flashing lights of automatic barriers provide the only contrasting colour against a treeless brown and green landscape, the true vastness of the Fens begins to sink in. But surprise is never very far away and at March it comes in the most unexpected of guises – a railway centre, or rather, a former railway centre. It doesn't take much stretch of the imagination to look around the seven echoing and largely empty platforms to see again the Victorian glory of this once-proud Great Eastern Railway station. From here, even in the 1960s, it would have been possible to travel south to St Ives, north to Wisbech, and north-west to Spalding; this last destination, indeed, losing its direct link as recently as 1982. All that remains now is the east–west connection from Peterborough to Ely, the 'strategic corridor' that we travel along today, the thriving goods link to Wisbech, and the Whitemoor marshalling yards.

The development and growth of March shows how communities have spread to meet the communications networks that serve them. Nearly three-quarters of a mile south of the station, straddling both sides of the Old River Nene, lies the town's present centre.

Here amid the commercial centre of customary small shops and chain stores will be found the charming Nene Parade, the centuries-old Griffin Hotel, and a thriving little market. From the centre, a pleasant riverside path will lead the walker beside weeping willows to the West End town park. This is March (its etymology shows a link with the 'marches' or border lands between England and Wales), but it is not

11

old March. The original town settlement was yet another mile farther south. Here, way beyond an ancient roadside cross, will be found the Parish Church of St Wendreda, with its carved double hammer-beam roof that led Sir Nikolaus Pevsner to declare that it has 'the most splendid timber roof in Cambridgeshire'. Even before this, on a walking tour of the region, the young composer and musician Gerald Finzi visited the church and later wrote, 'looking up at the double hammer-beam roof and the rows of carved *angels* . . . gave the feeling of a Botticelli Nativity . . . static from the very ecstasy'; yet in spite of this, local wits will doubtless be pleased to point out to you the lone carved devil that can be found amid so many heavenly, winged messengers!

Before we continue our train journey towards Ely, we might just catch a glimpse of a freight train taking the March west curve into the Whitemoor marshalling yards, or a light engine coming under the Norwood Road bridge from the locomotive depot. The sights, and the inevitable crew-change by the footbridge, serve as reminders of March's railway history. Though much freight-sorting is now done at New England, Peterborough, the cluster of small boys gathered in Norwood Road testifies that there are still sparks of life left in what was once Europe's largest marshalling yard. Skirting the eastern edge of March, the sharp-eyed traveller will be able to discern the former line to Chatteris and St Ives, then his own train heads out once more across miles of deserted fenland.

Between March and Ely, only one station remains open to a handful of local stopping trains, and this is Manea (pronounce it to rhyme with 'rainy'). Here there is a pair of raised platforms and a signal-box on the edge of the village. Local people who can remember at first hand the Transport Users' Consultative Committee closure inquiries of the 1960s will tell you that British Rail was not allowed to close Manea on account of the isolated nature of the community it serves.

In the event of flooding, the village's uncertain links with the rest of the world were deemed best served by train. Having no eastern access except by train, reason was seen, good sense prevailed, and Manea remains. Its desolation is Cambridgeshire fen at its most typical. Nevertheless, in pre-Beeching years, Manea found company in a handful of evocatively named, equally deserted but enchanting locations. On this line there were Stonea and Black Bank; farther afield Smeeth Road and Middle Drove.

The long straight run now to Ely has yet another surprise for us on this unadventurous line that has a knack of springing surprises. To see it at its most striking, travel in winter, at night, when there's a full moon. Beyond Manea you will cross the Hundred-Foot Washes which, when in full flood, will produce the illusion of crossing the sea. In its predominant colours of gunmetal grey, silver and, black, the ghostly water-scape with reflected moon will combine with the roar of train wheels on the raised viaduct to make you think you've left land for good on an inexorable run to the edge of the world. What it must have felt like for early travellers we can only imagine, but when the land was expertly drained the five-eighth mile between the Old and New Bedford Rivers was left as 'overspill' for the Wash. When this comes, in winter-time, the railway is the only crossing-place between Mepal and Downham Market.

Now through the site of two more closed stations, past the storage depot at Chettisham, our train takes us to within striking distance of the city of Ely. The cathedral has been visible for some time but now, suddenly, there are tracks all around us, as lines from King's Lynn and Norwich converge at Ely North Junction. The journey, without breaks, takes only forty minutes, we have left Peterborough a mere thirty miles away, but in that time we have traversed the centuries and experienced at first hand the expertise of the early railway engineers.

HITCHIN–CAMBRIDGE

by Mike Hadley

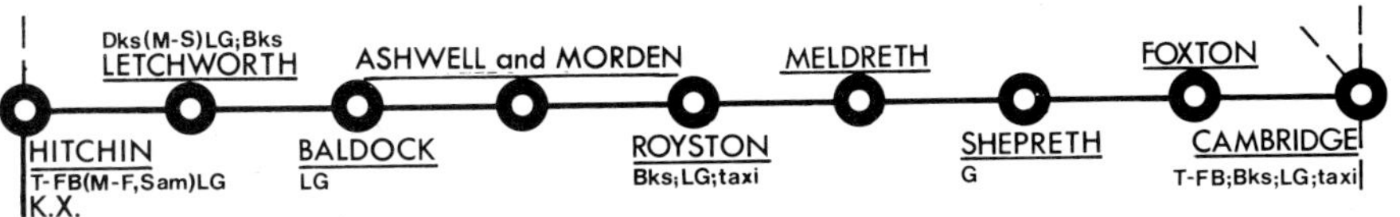

By means of a junction at Hitchin, the rail-traveller may gain access to East Anglia along the Great Northern route to Cambridge. Better known as a busy commuter route, this twenty-two-mile line gives access to the attractive belt of North Hertfordshire countryside which gradually gives way to the flatter more rural landscape associated with East Anglia. Nine towns and villages are served with a host of other villages close by. At one time the line was to be extended from Hitchin to Oxford, but permission was refused and only the section from Shepreth to Hitchin was specifically built as part of that cross-country route. Historians visiting the area can still see evidence of the custom anticipated at Letchworth Station: essentially an island station intended to have four tracks, enabling interchange between trains bound for London or Oxford. Earthworks to the west end of the cutting into Letchworth show how a line would also have diverged in the direction of Bedford.

Today two very different types of train operate the line: one using electric traction, and the other a more traditional diesel railcar which works the shuttle from Royston to Cambridge. The electric section from London ends at Royston and everyone must change here into the diesel train. The potential for holiday-makers using the line is considerable, in both town and country.

Hitchin is a market town and on a Saturday many bargains and surprises may be found among the stalls set out close to St Mary's Church. Nearby at Paynes Park an interesting collection of 'realia', paintings, and drawings associated with the town's history, can be found at the Museum and Art Gallery. The town is well endowed with public houses, shops, and one or two eating-places. For the energetic, short, medium, and long-distance walks are rewarding in all directions from Hitchin. If you have a foldaway bicycle some very rewarding rural rides are possible from the station out to the Hertfordshire villages of St Ipolytts, Gosmore, and Ickleford. Hitchin Station is an interchange junction offering scope for rail trips along the main line, northwards to Peterborough or southwards to the county town of Hertford or Hatfield and beyond.

On line in a north-easterly direction from Hitchin is situated the world's first Garden City at Letchworth. Here can be found a host of attractions and facilities, not least of these being the Garden City itself with its conservation sites – an interesting blend of town and country. Tree-lined avenues and roads, flanked by white pebble-dash cottages reveal the quality of early town planning. A visit on any weekday to the offices of the Garden City Corporation opposite the station, will enable one to obtain a guide – *Letchworth Achievement* – showing all conservation areas in the Garden City. A pleasant walk down Cowslip Hill and Wilbury Road leads to Standalone Farm, a Garden City Enterprise for all the family. Essentially a working farm, its 170 acres was planned from the outset in 1980 to cater for visitors; a large variety of livestock, farming equipment, and a wildfowl area awaits them. The hides are even equipped to take wheelchairs for the disabled.

Letchworth facilities include a market, hotels, shops, restaurants, a sports and

A refurbished DMU train provides the interim Royston–Cambridge connection – a mainline reduced to branchline status. (*Photo:* J. A. Howie)

leisure centre, indoor and outdoor swimming-pools, a cinema, and a theatre. Close to the station is Norton Common, a natural beauty-spot in the town, where the famous Letchworth black squirrels can be found. A good rail to bus interchange can be made here also with direct buses (Nos. 94 and 97) to Stotfold and Luton. There is also a direct Premier Travel Coach service to Oxford, and all buses run from or to points very near the railway station. Walkers from Letchworth to Baldock will be rewarded if they go via Norton Way North to Norton and Norton Bury before completing their walk at Baldock Station – approximately three miles.

Travelling from Letchworth to Baldock by train is a short hop, and Baldock Station is easily reached by trains from all points along the line. An evening out for drinks or food can easily be accommodated in Baldock. The town boasts an excellent wine bar and restaurant, a huge fish and chip shop and café, with several High Street cafés. The availability of food and drink here dates back to the coaching days before the Age of the Train. Walkers with architectural interests must inspect the church and some interesting buildings in the High Street and for those prepared to go farther afield, the nearby villages of Radwell, Sandon, and Wallington are worth a visit. This last village, and the farm half-way up the hill, are reputed to be the setting for George Orwell's *Animal Farm*.

Ashwell and Morden Station, situated at Odsey, serves Ashwell, Steeple, and Guilden Morden. It is a predominantly rural area and picturesque with its station nestling in a cutting surrounded by fields and a scatter of buildings. For absolute convenience, the Jester public house at the station gates is ideal for food, drink, and overnight accommodation or a longer stay. Two trains hourly call here in both directions, and this is a good starting-point for rambling, or if equipped with foldaway cycles, numerous country rides. Ashwell is two miles from the station, and worth visiting for its beautiful rural charm and architecture – and not forgetting the Seven Springs Gallery for that little gift.

Royston serves as terminus for the electric trains running north and the diesel railcars running south. The station was rebuilt when electrification reached the town in 1977. While there is no junction this strange interchange station, necessitated by the 'wires' ending here, conveys the atmosphere of a country junction of years ago. The immediate landscape around Royston is attractive, although somewhat scarred recently by the town's by-pass, relieving the centre which retains its country-town atmosphere. Royston has a market, some interesting back streets, and the nearby open space of Therfield Heath, easily reached on foot. From the highest point on the heath magnificent views across country enable distant Letchworth and Cambridge to be visible as well as the Bedfordshire countryside. Those interested in a circular rail tour can travel from Royston via Cambridge, Ely, and Peterborough and thence via Huntingdon and Hitchin back to Royston, perhaps spending a little time during the day to look at one or more of the places *en route*.

After departure from Royston the first village halt is at Meldreth where a more leisurely feel to the way of life is noticeable. One senses that East Anglia proper has been reached as the diesel railcars make their way through the Cambridgeshire countryside. The halts at Meldreth, Shepreth, and Foxton serve as launching pads for a series of cycle tours or walks to several small villages. A visit to Melbourn Apples at Meldreth is a must where, in a friendly atmosphere, fresh apples of every kind may be obtained along with other local produce. Melbourn and its surroundings reveal several examples of interesting architecture, before the return to the station and the train to Shepreth.

No visit to this area would be complete without a look at the expanding gardens around the crossing keeper's house, the crossing, and indeed the trackside at Shepreth. Of the two crossings we seek the one a few hundred yards south of the station. Walk from the station into the village, taking the first main road to the right towards the railway. The gardens and house are ahead on the right side of the road. From humble beginnings this garden, which is open to the public, has developed into a tourist attraction. A glance from the train window on arrival gives an indication of the extent of Mrs Fuller's work, which is now approaching the station itself. Waterfalls, ornaments of railway origin, and flowers, shrubs, etc. blend to form a traditional railway atmosphere in a highly original way.

Finally no visit to this area would be complete without getting off the train at Foxton. However, before coming read *The Common Stream* by Rowland Parker. Described as 'Two thousand years of the English Village', this book is reputed to reveal more about the history of Foxton than is known about any other like village in England. On arrival make sure the book is handy as it can be used on a village walkabout of two or three hours. The villagers are friendly, and their houses are a delight to the eye. A five-minute walk from the station takes one to the village centre and the church. There is much to be found on the surface and much more if you scratch it.

Close to Foxton Station, on the Cambridge side of the railway line, a Little Chef Restaurant can offer a quick and hearty meal for those who arrive tired and hungry. After passing Foxton the train does not stop again until arrival at Cambridge for connections deeper into East Anglia. The route previously covered is both fascinating and rewarding, with accommodation available at all points from Hitchin to Royston, enabling one to take in the delights of the countryside and use the various facilities and creature comforts of the larger towns. It is inevitable that more is left out than can be included. There is no substitute for a visit to discover this relatively unexplored area. Be sure to bring along maps, binoculars, camera, and *British Rail Timetable No. 25*, to explore, examine, and record the delights along the Great Northern.

HITCHIN–PETERBOROUGH

by Mike Hadley

Forty-four miles of railway between Hitchin and Peterborough form part of British Rail's East Coast Main Line, running from London to Edinburgh. Railway historians will know this route as the stamping-ground of the world-famous locomotive *Mallard* which broke the world speed record for steam in 1938, and the famous express train *Flying Scotsman*. Today, more than ever before, this line is host to some of Britain's fastest trains, and modern travellers this way can be forgiven if they have missed or are unfamiliar with the intermediate points of interest between Hitchin and Peterborough.

Predominantly rural, the area surrounding this stretch of line is also served by local trains which start at Hitchin. These services operate like those on a quiet country branch line but are well patronised by local people. The line skirts the western edge of East Anglia, serving the communities at and surrounding Biggleswade, Sandy, St Neots, Huntingdon, and the railway interchange at Peterborough. For the travellers from the south, this area is the first large open stretch of countryside after London's outer suburbia.

Running hourly from Hitchin, and every two hours on Sundays, the stopping trains connect with services from the Hertford branch and London's King's Cross Station to the south and from Cambridge to the north-east. Connections can also be made from the Nos. 93 and 94 United Counties buses from Luton to the west, which leave on the hour and set down across the road from Hitchin Station. After departure from Hitchin, passengers can see the Cambridge line branch out to the right, and the remains of the one-time Midland line from Sheffield via Bedford can be seen on the left.

A mile or so from the station the line crosses an old Roman road, the Icknield Way, at what used to be Cadwell crossing. This once busy east–west thoroughfare is now reduced to a narrow but pleasant footpath. For the energetic, it is possible to walk to this and along it from Hitchin Station via the village of Ickleford to Letchworth. Shortly after Cadwell we find buildings appearing to our right, which herald the start of England's longest village at Arlesey. Famous for its yellow bricks Arlesey is an interesting place for the rail-borne cyclist to visit (and a possible candidate for a reopened station). Behind the village the 'Blue Lagoon' can be found and used for picnics, while watching inland yachtsmen putting their craft through their paces. The water always seems bright and very blue, and set under yellow cliffs. It is all artificial, but due to its age nature has decorated man's work in such a way as to have made this a favourite picnic spot for many local people for decades. Disused clay workings which subsequently flooded were responsible, but they are well worth a visit.

Shortly after the train passes Arlesey it reaches Biggleswade and the first stop. A pleasant market town with small shops and restaurants, this makes an ideal start for a riverside walk to Sandy, some three miles away. The walk can be made from either town to the other, where there are connecting trains. Both Biggleswade and Sandy clearly depended on river traffic for their earlier trade, and evidence of this can be clearly seen along the river banks. Allow two or three hours for the walk, as there are interesting things to see. Biggleswade has some interesting architecture, though predominantly of the nineteenth century. This is ideal country for those equipped with bicycles, there being plenty of good country rides. The nearby aircraft museum at Old Warden is served by an infrequent Biggleswade–Bedford bus service, and flying days here are obviously a must.

The train ride from Biggleswade to Sandy takes only three or four minutes, but the rail-rider is presented with a pleasant view of Sandy Heath to the right. The BBC transmitter sits on the top, it being the highest point. Red rock peeps out between the vegetation, and the ridge is surrounded by lanes giving pleasant walks near by. Sandy itself is very small, but it is a friendly and pleasant place, with a good hourly bus service to Bedford from the square, a five- to ten-minute walk from the station. This was once a busy rail interchange for passengers and freight, with a line from Cambridge to Oxford sharing the station – yet another once-busy east–west thoroughfare which gave access to Bedford, and now in part footpath but in the main overgrown or built upon.

Sandy is famous now for Sandy Lodge, the home of the Royal Society for the Protection of Birds. Open to the public and not too far out of the town, it is as well to check with the RSPB for days and hours of opening. This is also an ideal starting station for those who carry foldaway bicycles. Bedford can be reached in half an hour's steady riding westwards; and to the east is a super cycle trip to Ashwell via Potton, Wrestlingworth, Guilden Morden, and Steeple Morden. This cycle ride has the advantage of ending up at Ashwell Station, where trains to Hitchin and connections back to Sandy can be made. Ordnance Survey Map No. 153 in the 1:50 000 First Series is an essential.

After Sandy the trains call at St Neots, where more riverside walks can be made. A pleasant market town with some impressive old brewery buildings, St Neots is fairly big, especially after Sandy. Shops, pubs, and places to eat are plentiful. Set on the River Great Ouse, which meanders its way from Bedford to Ely, St Neots enjoys a river-bus service to Bedford at certain times of year and day and this is certainly a quiet way to travel. The railway station is about fifteen minutes' walk from the town centre and riverside. For the cyclist arriving by rail who wants to 'get away from it all', a super circular ride can be made from the station via Staughton Green to West Perry and Grafham Water, and thence via Buckden, Offord Darcy, and Great Paxton to St Neots again. For those interested in church buildings, a visit to Hail Weston is rewarding as the tower is made with a wooden-brick effect and is most unusual.

Seven miles farther north the train calls at Huntingdon, and indeed many terminate here before going back to Hitchin. Passengers going on to Peterborough normally change into Inter-City trains, although a few trains from Hitchin do carry on to Peterborough at certain times. *British Rail Timetable No. 25* and *No. 26* are advisable to ascertain connections.

The town of Huntingdon has plenty to interest the visitor through its associations with Cromwell, and at nearby Brampton Pepys's house can be seen. Museums, shops, and restaurants are available, and again river walks. There are footpaths (see the Ordnance Survey Map mentioned above) which lead from near the station across to Godmanchester, a beautiful and very English village where rowing-boats can be hired for a quiet hour on the water. Huntingdon and its surrounding area are dotted with beautiful buildings, including the castellated one seen on the hill on the left as the train approaches Huntingdon Station. Finally, for the passengers who have their bicycles with them, no visit would be complete without a ride to the beautiful village of Buckden with its palace, *en route* to

High Speed Trains like this one, running at up to 125 mph, serve Stevenage, Huntingdon and Peterborough. (*Photo:* J. A. Howie)

Grafham Water and its bird reserves. From Grafham the cyclist can either return to Huntingdon or pedal south to St Neots Station by way of West Perry and Staughton Green.

For the non-cyclist, Huntingdon Bus Station is about five minutes' walk from the rail station across the riverside meadows. From there, buses run hourly to St Ives (serving both sides of the River Great Ouse and some exceptionally pretty villages), Cambridge, St Neots or Bedford (also serving some attractive Ouse Valley villages), and Peterborough. The last of these passes the air base at Alconbury and the village of Stilton, which gave its name to the cheese that was originally sold there. A less frequent service runs to Ramsay with its National Trust abbey gatehouse.

It must be said that, while specific items and places are at times few and far between in this part of England, simply being in it and the fresh air can be enough to refresh those parts which other places never reach. A good foldaway bicycle can certainly enhance the pleasure of being here, as well as giving access to places where other road vehicles often cannot go. Cycle hire in the area is generally poor, but researches into local bus timetables will certainly extend the possibilities for exploration.

After a change of train at Huntingdon, we are swiftly transported the remaining seventeen and a half miles, mainly across open fens, to Peterborough and its important rail interchange station. Connections to most parts of Britain can be made here, including direct trains to Birmingham, Sheffield, Norwich, Cambridge, Harwich, London, and Edinburgh. Peterborough is by far the largest place along our route, and it is a city. A vast new traffic-free shopping area close to the station makes this an ideal place for a spending spree. In recent years locals have given up their pilgrimage to London in favour of Peterborough. A visit to the cathedral is a must, as indeed is a trip to the Nene Valley Railway – a very well-managed line with plenty to interest old and young alike in addition to being an excellent public service.

Accommodation along the route from Hitchin to Peterborough is available more easily at the larger places, Peterborough, St Neots, or Huntingdon. There are camping facilities at Nene Park, and most places have bed and breakfast facilities. Clearly for the rail-based tourist, the line is better explored than passed by on fast Inter-City services. However, when leaving for the north and/or home, Inter-City trains can be boarded at Stevenage (a few miles south of Hitchin), Huntingdon, or Peterborough.

NENE VALLEY STEAM RAILWAY

by John Goose

Peterborough's first railway, opened on 2 June 1845, ran along the Nene Valley to Northampton. British Rail closed the route to passengers in 1964 and to freight in 1972; but total closure was short-lived, for from 1 June 1977 a passenger timetable again operated from Orton Mere, on the edge of the city,. to Wansford. The Peterborough Railway Society had persuaded the city's Development Corporation to purchase six miles of trackbed so that a steam railway could enhance the Nene Park Leisure Area.

Wansford Station, by the A1 road at Stibbington, became the railway's headquarters. The main building is from nearby Barnwell and has been reconstructed. There is a small turntable, an attractive footbridge, locomotive sheds, a museum, a shop, refreshment carriages, and the longest fully equipped preserved signal-box in Britain on the site. Many of the score of steam locomotives, as many carriages, and half a dozen diesels to be seen are of continental origin, for uniquely in Britain the line operates to the Berne loading gauge. British locomotives usually present are the Class 7 *Britannia*, Class 5 *City of Peterborough*, 'Battle of Britain' *92 Squadron*, Deltic D9000, 55022 *Royal Scots Grey*, and a tank engine officially named by the Reverend W. Awdry as *Thomas*.

Since September 1983 journeys westward beneath the A1 and through the 616-yard-long Wansford Tunnel have become possible to Yarwell Mill, an attractive stretch of the Nene with its water-mill, touring caravan park, and flooded excavation pits. Here there is no public access and our locomotive must run round at the old junction of the routes from Northampton and Rugby, the nearby bridges having been removed on both.

Eastwards from Wansford, the Nene lies south of the railway, and the trackbed of the old Stamford and Essendine branch closed in 1931 curves away to the north. Soon the site of Castor Station, perhaps a later rebuilding project, appears and opposite, beyond the river, the village of Water Newton with, farther on, the site of Durrobrivae, a Roman town which straddled Ermine Street. On crossing the Nene one then enters the centrepiece of this whole amenity area, Ferry Meadows Country Park. Based on attractive lakes in a curve of the river, it offers every imaginable water sport and pastime, nature reserves, riding, caravanning, golf, a trim track, adventure playgrounds, a miniature railway, an information centre and café, and extensive walks. Ferry Meadows Station with its interesting platform murals stands at the park entrance.

Eventually the railway runs close by the river at Orton Staunch with its lock-gate and pleasure craft. Here Orton Mere Station, a new brick building in traditional style and with sales facilities, is accompanied by a signal-cabin and run-round loop, for this is the present limit of services. Trackwork, however, continues beneath a massive road bridge to Longueville Junction and the link with British Rail's Fletton Loop from the main line to the nearby sugar-beet factory. British Rail has run diesel multiple units along this route on summer Saturdays to link

Peterborough mainline station with Orton Mere. Eastern Counties buses also operate from the Queensgate Centre, Peterborough past Orton Mere Station. (For details telephone Peterborough Bus Station – Peterborough 54571.)

Recently Longueville has become a true junction once again with trackwork relaid eastwards beside the Nene for a further one and a half miles to where it formerly joined the Peterborough–March route beneath the East Coast Main Line. No new connection is planned, but the Nene Valley Railway hopes, in 1986, to open its 'Peterborough Nene Valley Station' here on the site of the former London & North Western Railway engine-shed. This station development, eventually with full facilities, close to the city centre, and with ready access from the spacious Oundle Road Car Park and surrounding meadows, may well begin to offer the Peterborough Railway Society a realistic chance of pursuing its ultimate goal of establishing a 'Museum of World Railways' akin to the National Railway Museum at York.

ELY–KING'S LYNN

by Chris Milnes

The twenty-six-mile Ely to King's Lynn Railway is operated by Inter-City-type trains, though the line itself is part of the provincial services network and has to be supported by the Passenger Service Obligation grant aid system, which had its origins in the 1968 Transport Act, to keep essential rail links open.

This rail line is an important link for the area, and the trains are relatively well used, despite a fairly leisurely average speed of about 45 mph.

The trains are formed of hauled coaching stock of the 'Mk 2' type, and some compartment stock is still used on the line. There are first-class facilities, and plenty of van space for bicycles, prams, etc., an important asset for people shopping or touring by bicycle.

Most trains have a buffet facility, mainly the miniature buffet system of drinks, sandwiches, etc., but no hot meals.

We begin our journey at Ely, a largish station, which will be modernised in the near future as part of the Cambridge area colour light signalling scheme. The train runs past a picturesque marina and the Maltings, a large building now used as a meeting-place, with the cathedral dominating the skyline. After the marina we pass over the Kiln Lane level crossing; on the left are flooded gravel workings, now a mini bird sanctuary. At Ely North Junction the line branches into three routes: one to March, one to Norwich, and the middle one to King's Lynn. We pass through undulating farmland for about five miles, until a caravan site next to a river bank on the right heralds the train's arrival at Littleport. We pass over Sandhills level crossing and a quarter of a mile farther on reach Littleport Station, now an unstaffed halt. The centre of Littleport is about one mile's walk from the station and has a few small shops. Near to the station is a boatyard and a restaurant.

North of Littleport the railway becomes single track, and we pass over Littleport By-pass level crossing under construction. The countryside becomes flatter and the soil blacker, typical Fen country. The single line has recently been relaid with deep limestone ballast to improve track stability. Subsidence is a great problem for Fenland railways, caused by peat first drying out and shrinking and then swelling in wet weather. We gather speed and pass the site of Black Horse Drove, and then Southery goods sidings, closed in 1964. Two miles farther on at Hilgay, an automatic crossing over a single-track road is all that remains of the station, axed in 1964. The train slows to a 20 mph subsidence speed restriction over the bridge crossing the River Great Ouse, another part of the network needing investment. We then accelerate past the site of Denver Junction, where the Stoke Ferry branch used to join our line on the right. The Stoke Ferry line lost its passengers in 1930 and its freight in 1965. Occasional freight trains continued to operate down to the British Sugar Corporation's refinery at Wissington, but even these ceased in 1981 when bridges were found to be unable to take modern freight stock axle weights.

Denver signal-box has recently been closed and the crossing automated. The former signal-box nameboard was sold on a television programme for a Children in Need charity fund-raising operation.

Two miles farther on is Downham Market, a small town whose attractive station building is of carrstone, a local material. The local Amenity Society has in recent years provided plants and shrubs as well as improved station signs. A short walk away is the town centre, which has a small shopping arcade and some nice pubs, as well as an attractive black and white clock-tower. North from Downham Market the line runs alongside the River Great Ouse, which flows behind a high bank. Stow Gate box, on our left, marks the site of a station serving Stow Bardolph until 1964. After passing Holme Road level crossing our train slows to enter Magdalen Road Station, once a junction for the March line. This station, closed in 1968, was reopened in 1975 after local people had clubbed together and raised money to this end. Only minor modifications such as new signs, fencing, and electric lighting were needed. It serves the villages of Watlington to the east and Wiggenhall St Mary Magdalen to the west. Five miles beyond Magdalen Road we approach King's Lynn; at Harbour Junction lines branch off to serve Campbell's Soups, British Sugar Corporation, and Dalgety private sidings. The signal-box at Harbour Junction has recently been closed and points are now electrically operated from King's Lynn junction box, part of an on-going modernisation scheme, which will also see the automation of the level crossing at Extons Road a half a mile to the north. Our train slows as we pass redundant Extons Road sidings, allotments and factories, backing on to the railway line.

At Tennison Avenue level crossing note on your right a single-track branch line, formerly the King's Lynn–Dereham line, now surviving as a freight-only route to the British Industrial sand workings at Middleton Towers, three miles from King's Lynn. We are then drawing into the fairly spacious station, which is also the railhead for the Royal Family when they visit their home at Sandringham.

King's Lynn is a busy rail freight centre, the main traffic being white silica sand transported to Yorkshire for glass-making. Other commodities handled are chemicals to the Dow chemical factory. Canned food is sent by Speedlink fast freight services to Scotland. Grain is often handled in large quantities. The British Sugar Corporation also sends out much van traffic and receives limestone and oil. Recent new traffic has been new Skoda motor cars by the trainload, and container trains for the docks. King's Lynn town centre is only a quarter of a mile to the west of the station and has a busy expanding shopping centre with many large chain stores. A recent new development is Westgate House, a new large clothes store next to the bus station. Adjacent to the railway station is a large Texas Homecare superstore. The busy town contains many interesting old buildings, the Tuesday

Marketplace being very attractive. Several of the old quayside buildings are being renovated and there are many interesting side streets and river banks to investigate. The bus and coach station is near to the shopping centre, a few minutes' walk from the railway station. Local bus services operated by Eastern Counties include a half-hourly link to Hunstanton, travelling through picturesque Sandringham and Castle Rising. Hourly buses run via Holbeach to Spalding, a route worth travelling during the tulip season. Buses also serve Cromer via Fakenham and Norwich via Swaffham.

The future of the King's Lynn to Ely rail link looks brighter, especially as railways are reducing operating costs and administration drastically and the King's Lynn line has already been extensively rationalised. Cutting costs and introducing new technology has helped the railways to gain new traffic flows, and King's Lynn is a good example of this trend. West Norfolk felt the full effects of the Beeching closures, all the local paytrain system operating from King's Lynn having been shut down in 1968–69. However, the Magdalen Road reopening helped set the more recent trend of reopening axed stations, and building new ones in conurbations. Such low-cost reopening, often done by self-help from the public and local authorities, is being copied in many places throughout the United Kingdom.

PETERBOROUGH–KING'S LYNN RAIL LINK COACH

by John Goose

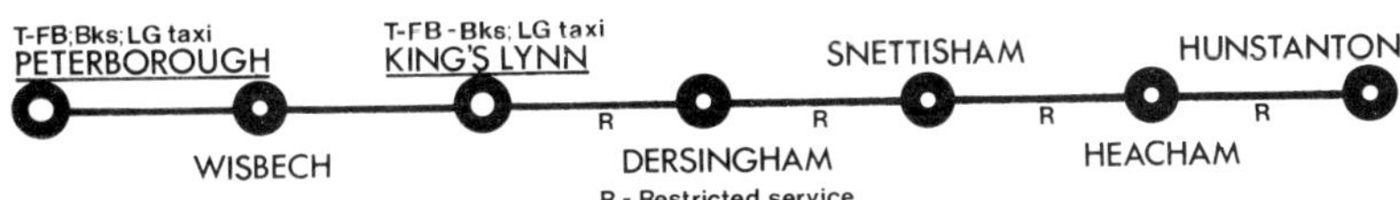

Since 17 May 1982, the holder of a rail ticket to King's Lynn has, at certain times of day, been able to leave Peterborough Station from its 'extra platform' on the forecourt. There, under the shadow of the impressive and enlarged Great Northern Hotel, we are confronted with a coach which, in its blue and grey livery and with its British Rail logo, is perhaps striving to look like a train. As well as serving Wisbech and King's Lynn, the coach now also runs once a day through to Hunstanton, which lost its rail service fifteen years ago.

The Rail Link Coach starts on its journey through the city of Peterborough and the village of Eye, then across the level Fens on long straight roads made possible by the chequered field patterns of the flat landscape. The equally straight course of the former Midland & Great Northern Joint Railway (closed to passengers in 1959 and subsequently to freight) can be seen as if a ghost from the past running to the north of the road.

At Guyhirn the coach passes under the bridge of the March–Spalding line (closed in November 1982), turning sharply to the right over the River Nene, whose banks we follow closely to Wisbech.

Wisbech is served by rail, with the branch from March carrying increasing amounts of freight – coal, metal, pet food, occasionally seed potatoes and steel coil,

23

and potentially increasing quantities of grain. The passenger service ceased in 1968, but since 1978 six successful passenger excursions have been run, on the initiative of the Railway Development Society, carrying local people to Cambridge for shopping (three times) and to the seaside resorts of Lowestoft, Felixstowe, and Scarborough.

With their Rail Link Coach service, British Rail would seem to be conceding that Wisbech has a population large enough to deserve a rail link (no larger town in East Anglia is without one); or at least that a more direct east–west route from North Norfolk to Peterborough, the Midlands, and the North should have been retained.

Wisbech is the coach's only scheduled intermediate stop. Its many notable buildings include the magnificent Georgian Brinks alongside the river, Elgoods' Brewery, Peckover House (built in 1722 for a local banking family, now a Grade I listed building open to the public and in the care of the National Trust), the old Grammar School, the seventy-foot-high Clarkson Memorial, and the Crescent with its oval of Georgian town houses on the site of the former castle. The museum, parish church, inns and market, are all worth a visit.

Our coach heads on towards King's Lynn, and is soon again among flat arable fields, but in a perhaps rather more mature landscape, where the road is not so straight at times, some of the houses are more ancient, and the landscape is dotted with several fine churches.

Approaching the River Great Ouse, the large towers and tanks of the King's Lynn sugar-beet factory can be seen on the far bank. We cross the river on a new bridge virtually at the point where the Midland & Great Northern Joint Railway bridge once stood. Storage sidings and a coal depot stand where South Lynn Station used to be – this freight spur being one of the few short stretches of the M&GN still in use.

We begin to thread our way through the streets of the ancient and venerable port of King's Lynn. As if to emphasise the town's past grandeur, we still must pass through the South Gate, built not for defence but, in 1440, as an example of civic pride.

A turn to the right soon brings us into the forecourt of King's Lynn railway station, and the traveller is once again in touch with the Inter-City passenger network. Here are two hostelries – The Greyfriars and the East Anglian Hotel (the latter still proudly proclaiming itself a 'posting establishment') – to welcome the weary Rail Link Coach traveller; for one thing our coach could not provide, in its strenuous efforts to be a train of the road, was a buffet!

Some fine Norfolk flintwork in the Trinity Guildhall, one of King's Lynn's historic buildings.

ST EDMUNDS LINE

by John Brodribb

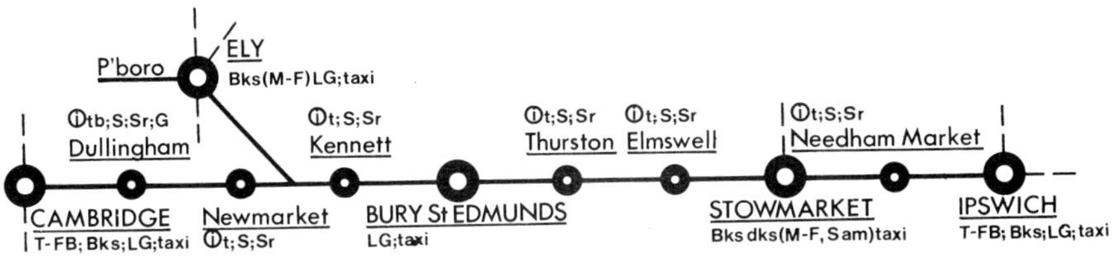

The St Edmunds line of British Rail joins several important cities and towns, notably Cambridge, Ely, Bury St Edmunds, Newmarket, Stowmarket, and Ipswich, and serves a number of other small communities as well. In addition to the purely local services, the route, opened between 1846 and 1854, also provides through services between East Anglia and the rest of the country, with a variety of connections at Cambridge and Peterborough.

Cambridge Station is some way from the city centre, although there is a frequent bus service between the two. There is a good street plan in the station booking-hall, and while the Travel Centre sells the official tourist guide, it is worth going to the Tourist Office, off Market Hill, which has a very good range of maps and guides. Cambridge Station is unusual in having only one long main platform, although local services start from bay platforms at either end. St Edmunds line trains usually leave from one such at the north end, and soon diverge from the main line towards the east.

After clearing the suburbs of Cambridge the line climbs to pass the site of Fulbourne Station, and traverses open arable country before woodland heralds the approach to Dullingham Station, some eleven miles out. It is a quiet spot, and the traveller alighting here can watch the train disappear into the distance while the signalman closes the level-crossing gates behind it. The village is about ten minutes' walk along the lane, and a further ten minutes' stroll, past the grounds of Dullingham House, brings the church, village green, and two pubs into view.

The train-traveller will now be in Newmarket, a pleasant town famed as the home of the Jockey Club and Britain's main centre for the 'Sport of Kings'. The station building, a vast and splendid red-brick structure, is now used by a local company supplying the needs of horse-racing, and trains use the one remaining platform. The town centre is reached by turning right out of the station and left at the end of the road; Tattersalls' Sales Paddocks are on the way. There is a town map on the right as one enters the High Street, and a little farther along is the National Horse-racing Museum, a 'must' for anyone interested in the Turf. It is open from May to November; 10 am to 5 pm Tuesday to Saturday and 2 pm to 5 pm Sundays; closed Mondays except Bank Holidays.

On leaving Newmarket, the train passes grain silos and plunges into Warren Hill Tunnel (the longest in East Anglia) before emerging into deeply wooded surroundings. At Chippenham Junction the line from Ely joins from the left, and on the right racehorses can often be seen exercising. The A45 trunk road appears on the left, and from now on keeps close company with the train. Five miles from Newmarket is Kennett Station, serving the villages of Kennett and Kennett End. The weary traveller will find the Bell free house within ten minutes' walk – turn right out of the station. Still in close company with the A45, the line passes two small closed stations, one of which – Saxham and Risby (closed in 1967) – is the site of a large agricultural machinery depot.

At length, twenty-nine miles from Cambridge, the train pulls into Bury St Edmunds. The large station betrays a much busier past, although it is still an Inter-City stop, as befits a cathedral town which even has its own independent local radio station. There is much to see in Bury; the town centre is about twenty minutes' walk. Turn right out of the station drive and keep going in more or less a straight line; turn right at the lights. This will bring the visitor to Angel Corner, with the abbey and cathedral opposite; the National Trust Clock and Watch Exhibition adjacent (open free from May to October, 10 am to 1 pm and 2 pm to 5 pm); and the main shopping centre on the right. The Tourist Office, open only in the summer months, is just inside the abbey gateway.

Trains continue from Bury St Edmunds Station, crossing over the main Thetford road and the A45. Lines once diverged to both north and south here, but little trace of these now remains. Seven minutes' ride away is Thurston Station, which has been newly repainted, and which sports smart flower-beds tended by members of the local Women's Institute. Just outside is the Fox and Hounds pub, itself newly refurbished and reopened. Considerable housing developments have taken place here in recent years, some of which can be seen from the railway. It is a pleasant walk through the lanes to Elmswell, passing through the unspoilt village of Tostock, and although much of the countryside has been denuded of trees and hedges in the interests of greater agricultural efficiency, there are some pleasantly wooded parts.

Elmswell Station, seven minutes' ride from Thurston, is one of the smarter unstaffed halts in the county – its buildings, awning, signal-box, and level-crossing gates having fairly recently been repainted. It serves a large village, with pub and shops immediately by the station. The railway continues on its undulating way for a further three and a half miles before trains slow for Haughley Junction, where they join the main Norwich to Ipswich line. All trains from Ely and Cambridge call at the next station, Stowmarket, an elaborate 1849 edifice with shaped gables and angled towers. Within the past eighteen months British Rail have carried out extensive improvements here: both platforms have been extended and a new footbridge provided. New platform canopies and supporting columns have been built, which blend very well with the older parts. All this is in connection with the mainline electrification, signs of which are now very obvious on the journey southwards. Travelling on, there is one more stop before Ipswich, at Needham Market. The station here was closed in 1967, along with most other mainline stops not serving large towns, but was reopened in 1971; most of the local Cambridge trains call here. Ipswich is just over ten minutes away, with some services continuing to Harwich. Stowmarket and Needham Market are also on the Gipping Valley River Path, which gives a walk of some seventeen miles and starts near Ipswich Station. Suffolk County Council has erected a series of notice-boards showing water-mills, picnic sites, a nature reserve, and other amenities. It is a pleasant walk one way, possibly returning by train.

Travellers from the Midlands and North to East Anglia may well travel via March and Ely to reach the St Edmunds line, and the section between Ely and Chippenham Junction, opened in 1879, is very different in character from the other parts. Leaving Ely in a southerly direction, Ipswich trains diverge almost at once from the main line, and cross the River Great Ouse. Black fenland soil stretches away on both sides of the line into the distance. Look out for some of the less obvious crops: for carrots, onions, and many other vegetables are grown here. Trains do not stop until Bury St Edmunds, but the site of Soham Station is fairly clear. It is about five miles from Ely, and was the scene of remarkable heroism in the Second World War. In the small hours of 2 June 1944 the front wagon of an ammunition train caught fire near Soham. Showing incredible courage, Driver Benjamin Gimbert and Fireman James Nightall uncoupled the blazing van, loaded with forty 500 lb bombs, and were trying to get it clear of the town when it exploded in the station, killing the fireman and signalman, and badly injuring the driver. Driver Gimbert and Fireman Nightall were subsequently awarded the George Cross, and are each today commemorated on mainline locomotives which bear their names.

Fordham, the next station (closed in 1965), was the junction for Mildenhall; the trackbed of this branch can be seen on the left. Shortly afterwards the Snailwell Stud Farm can also be seen on the same side, with horses often being exercised. Chippenham Junction is soon passed, with the line from Cambridge and Newmarket joining from the right.

BRECKLAND LINE

by Gordon Knott

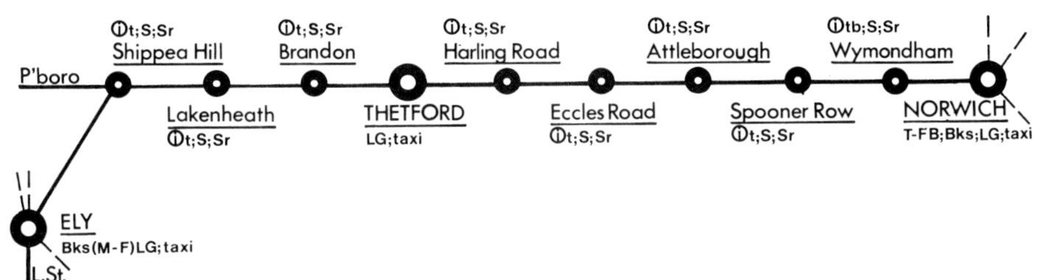

If you have made your way by train from Cambridge or Peterborough, by the time you reach Ely, you will have begun to wonder whether the scenery – a vast expanse of flat fenland – will ever change. If you take the Breckland line, it will have changed – not once, but several times and beautifully – and your small adventure will reward you.

Swinging away from Ely, you leave its grand cathedral and its boats on your left (if you are coming from March, on your right). After reflecting perhaps for a moment how those medieval men brought all that stone to a hill in the middle of a huge marsh, watch the lines to Peterborough and King's Lynn vanish to your left, and ride once more through the open fen with seemingly more celery than the world could possibly eat on either side. Look out for the otherwise unromantic Fenman's habit of growing masses of flowers round his house, and the numbers of pheasants which seem to ignore the passing trains, and before you know it you are at Shippea Hill. (What hill? You may well ask. In fact, the '-ea' at the end of the name, not unusual round here, indicates one of the old islands that stood up from the Fens.)

From this staging-point for many Americans on their way to the great bases at Lakenheath and Mildenhall, you can make your way by foot or cycle (but don't expect to find a bus!) to either of these places, with their fine angel-roofed churches.

If you stay on the train, you will pass through large, unusual groves of poplars, planted by a well-known match firm, and in five miles you will reach Lakenheath

Station. On for another five minutes to Brandon, and as you go the scenery begins to change for the first time. On your left, the River Little Ouse comes alongside, and from being little more than a Fenland dike becomes a real river of the kind that

At Brandon comes the second change, and you enter the Breckland from which the line takes its name. Once a great dust-bowl created by the foolish farming ways of our prehistoric ancestors, it became a vast heath covering many square miles, on which little grew except heather and scrub. Modern farming has now recovered much of it, and the Forestry Commission with their Thetford Forest have changed the face of that part which you are now entering.

Brandon itself is a pleasant, unpretentious Suffolk town with a number of good pubs. From here you can explore the forest which stretches for miles, follow the river to the beautifully set village of Santon Downham (but the best view of all is possibly from the train), or visit Grime's Graves, from which prehistoric men dug out flints for their implements.

It is seven miles to Thetford if you choose to walk or cycle (and the whole of the Breckland line runs through ideal cycling country, with few steep hills and many pleasant lanes), but the train will take you there in ten minutes or so. Before you leave the station, look at the unusual ironwork on the pillars supporting the platform awnings, with their railway motif. The largest town on the line, Thetford, is an Inter-City stop, and all fast trains to Norwich and Birmingham, as well as some summer holiday trains to Great Yarmouth, call here.

With its large London overspill estates and its new industries, Thetford has seen much change, but it is a town of great antiquity and well worth a visit. Its castle mound and priory and abbey ruins can easily be visited on foot, as can its shopping centre and pleasant riverside walks by the Little Ouse and Thet. There are several hotels in the town, and camping sites in the forest for the walker and cyclist. While you are there, don't forget to visit Kilverstone Wildlife Park, with its miniature studs, a mile and a half from the station in a beautiful woodland setting and a treat for the children.

On from Thetford through the forest again, and in about five minutes you will be crossing Roundham Heath and catch a glimpse of the Breckland that was, with heather, bracken, and scrub, on your way to Harling Road, a mile from the village of East Harling, which has a fine church and a pleasing little market-place with old houses. As you leave the heath the countryside undergoes its third change, and you enter the slightly rolling landscape of fields and trees typical of so much of Norfolk. Eccles Road Station serves the hamlets of Eccles and Quidenham, with their interesting little round-towered churches, of which Norfolk has so many. These bear witness to the inability of small parishes to pay the cost of importing stone and their manner of using local flint (which cannot be cut square) to the best advantage. Between Harling Road and Eccles Road, look out on your left for cars and motor cycles speeding round the Snetterton Racing Circuit (meetings from March until the end of October, at week-ends).

Attleborough is a small town on the main road from London to Norwich which has grown rapidly in recent years. Apart from the solid, squat parish church and the Griffin pub, it contains few buildings of great note, but as you enter the station look out for the huge piles of kegs and barrels which signal the large cider factory for which the town is known.

At Banham, some five miles from Attleborough (once more, don't expect to find a bus) you may sample many kinds of cider and local wines at a Cider House, or visit Banham Zoo, a well laid out local attraction.

It is quiet but pleasant country now all the way, and after passing Spooner Row,

Inter-City train on the Breckland line passing through Thetford Forest. (*Photo:* John C. Baker)

Ely Cathedral.

the smallest station on the line, look out on your left for the oddly assorted twin towers of Wymondham Abbey. Wymondham ('Windham' to the locals if you are asking for a ticket) is an attractive town, with narrow streets full of old houses, and a fine seventeenth-century market cross; it has a number of good shops and pubs and a visit to the town and abbey will repay the effort. Those interested in railways will have noted a single line coming in from the left, just before entering Wymondham Station: this is the freight-only line from Dereham, closed to passengers in 1969, but used by more than a dozen excursion trains since 1978.

You are now on the final stage of your journey to Norwich, the 'fine city' of which Cobbett wrote and of which its people are justly proud. As your train speeds down from Hethersett, do not miss Keswick water-mill on your right, just after you have crossed the River Yare for the first time. On down this small valley, your train runs through the water-meadows and under Harford Viaduct, which carries the main line from London; it drops down and joins the Breckland line just before the now disused Trowse Station. A swing bridge takes you over the River Wensum and you may catch, if you are lucky, a sight of one of the small coasters which still come up to Norwich from the sea. Norwich itself, with its infinite variety of things to do and see, then awaits you.

BROADS LINE

by Wallace Boyles

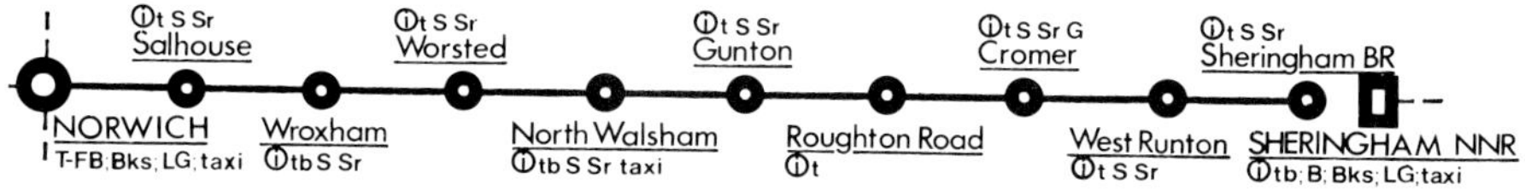

Norfolk is noted among other things for its profusion of churches – some of them 'pocket cathedrals' situated in tiny villages and small towns – and a series of shallow lakes locally known as 'Broads'. The latter, together with the connecting rivers, afford some 200 miles of navigable waters and attract thousands of tourists year after year.

The Broads are centred mainly on three rivers: the Yare, which empties into the sea at Great Yarmouth, the Waveney (partly in Suffolk), and the Bure, the last named joining the Yare within a short distance of Great Yarmouth.

The most important of the three, from the standpoint of the Broads, is the Bure, flowing through Wroxham, the most notable and popular of the Broadland centres. Wroxham is served by the line from Norwich to the resorts of Cromer and Sheringham, and it is this route which British Rail have named the 'Broads line'.

Broads line trains leave the Wherry line, one and three-quarter miles out of Norwich, at Whitlingham Junction and begin an initially steep ascent out of the Yare Valley, eventually to level out for a steady run to Salhouse, four miles distant. On the way we pass through the expanded village of Rackheath, whose inhabitants for many years past have yearned for a halt and who, wistfully perhaps, hear our klaxon as we approach the three automatic level crossings in the vicinity. The coal dump visible in the near distance on the left of the isolated station, serving the scattered village of Salhouse, marks the site of a large wartime bomber aerodrome

Norwich–Sheringham train descends Cromer ridge. (*Photo:* R. C. Vincent)

Cromer seafront.

On the River Bure at Wroxham.

of which little now remains.

Leaving Salhouse, we run smartly down a falling grade for the next two miles, passing numerous lineside dwellings before slowing as we rumble past the diminutive Bridge Broad and over the River Bure where a large and varied assortment of river craft, boatyards, and riverside buildings greet the eye before we come to a stand in Wroxham Station. Usually to be seen in the sidings are special wagons for the conveyance of barley for the Scotch whisky industry.

Wroxham (with neighbouring Hoveton) is today more than a centre for summer boating holidays. It is also a flourishing, modern all-year-round shopping centre, having developed tremendously since the days before the Second World War when it was reputed to possess the largest village store in the world.

On single line now for the rest of the journey, we surmount the stiff rise out of Wroxham and note, bearing away on the left, a cutting devoid of the iron road which once connected the villages and small towns of Central Norfolk. This line, from Wroxham to County School (on the Wymondham–Dereham–Wells-next-the-Sea line) via Aylsham and Reepham, closed to regular passenger trains as long ago as 1952, and more recently to freight traffic, but between 1976 and 1981 it was used by five excursion trains. Continuing, mainly on the level, through typical Norfolk arable land, we draw up six minutes later at Worstead where, close to the line on the left, is a large food-processing factory mostly screened by conifers.

In the twelfth century many wool-combers came over to England from Flanders and it was here at Worstead that the Flemings first settled and practised their craft. Their products came to be known as 'worsted' after the name of what in those far-off days was a prosperous town, but is now merely a village. In the summer each year an attractive three-day festival is held here.

Conspicuous half a mile to the right is the fine parish church with its lofty tower, now bereft of its stately pinnacles erected in 1844. The church, like that at North Walsham, our next stop, owes much to the weavers. As we tackle the sharp climb out of Worstead we notice, on the left, in the woodlands of Westwick Park, a circular observation tower, not unlike a lighthouse, rising well above the tree-tops, ninety feet high and over 200 years old. Some years ago, alas, the tower was denuded of its attractive windowed octagonal summit apartment which commanded a superb vista limited on the north and east by a large extent of coastline.

Approaching North Walsham, a thriving market town with light industry, an attractive shopping precinct, and a market cross dating back to 1550, we pass on one side a large rose nursery, very colourful, and on the other, parallel with us for some distance, a new road made on the bed of the former Midland & Great Northern Joint Railway (Great Yarmouth–Peterborough/Spalding–Bourne–Little Bytham), most of which was closed in 1959, its separate station in North Walsham now 'one with Nineveh and Tyre'.

In North Walsham sidings, on the right, are rail-tankers used for the transport of condensates, a by-product in the recovery of natural gas from the North Sea, which are fed to the sidings by a pipeline from the Bacton gas installations a few miles away on the coast. On the left is a large canning factory.

Immediately on leaving North Walsham we rumble over the Norwich main road and behold on the left the fine sports ground of the Paston School where Nelson was a pupil for two years. Founded in 1606 by Sir William Paston, the grammar school was greatly enlarged and extended between the world wars. Since the autumn of 1984 it has been functioning in its new role as a co-educational Sixth Form College.

The buildings can be glimpsed through the trees on the right, as can, and much more clearly, the ruined tower of the parish church, unusual in its shape and size, the second largest in Norfolk. Part of the tower fell down in 1724, another portion in 1835, and more the following year, when some of the remaining fragments, being in a dangerous state, were taken down. Further safety work on the tower was found necessary in 1939. Faulty construction and the elements account for the tower's unhappy history.

Moments later we are crossing another bridge, this one spanning the trackless bed of the M&GN Railway, affectionately known as the 'Muddle and Get Nowhere', whose trains at this point dived underneath on their way to North Norfolk's 'Little Crewe', the now defunct four-spoke hub of the joint railway situated at Melton Constable, seventeen miles westwards.

For some miles in that direction, the line today is part of what is known as Weavers' Way; though not a public right of way – as a local authority's lineside notice-board makes clear to the wanderer – 'residents and visitors are permitted to use it at their own risk as a footpath and bridleway'. Ideal for a carefree ramble far removed from careering cars and grinding, lumbering lorries.

So to Gunton, or rather the station so named. Gunton Station – two miles or so east of Gunton Hall, an eighteenth-century white-brick mansion at present being restored and converted into dwellings – is nearer to the sizeable village of Southrepps, visible on our right, with its church and lofty tower, when we draw out of the station. The spacious building on the west platform, once used by the landed gentry, today serves as a private house. Pot plants on the veranda and along the platform contribute to the traveller's enjoyment during the train's brief pause here. A few yards beyond the station is a public house, very convenient for those disposed to break their journey.

Now comes a switchback for close on four miles: a stiff climb, then gradually down, then sharply up again to reach the Cromer–Holt Ridge.

Prior to September 1954, trains from Norwich bound for Cromer ran into Cromer High, a windswept terminus situated on an escarpment high above the town roughly a mile away.

For reasons of rationalisation and to the greater convenience of most travellers, the station was closed and trains diverted to Cromer Beach, also a terminus but much nearer to the town centre and close to the seafront.

To reach this former M&GN station we veer to the left about three-quarters of a mile south of the now non-existent High Station, then, at reduced speed, turn sharply west just short of the elegant under-bridge at Roughton Road, the site of a new halt and where the coastal or 'Poppy' line to Overstrand, Sidestrand, and Mundesley-on-Sea (part of the old Norfolk & Suffolk Joint Railway closed in 1953) diverged and descended to tunnel under the old High Station goods yard. Roughton Road Halt, three miles by rail from Cromer Station, is pleasantly situated amid woodlands and very convenient for those Cromer residents in the south-east district of the resort where in recent years housing estates have been developed.

From here we hasten along embankments and through cuttings prettily wooded until the brakes go on as we prepare to make an inverted U-turn – from west to east – before descending slowly through a deep and winding cutting to draw up at one of the two platforms of the now unstaffed terminus. Ahead of us, from the main platform, we see the magnificent pinnacled tower of Cromer Parish Church rising to 160 feet, the highest in Norfolk and from which a light was nightly displayed on the seaward side before the erection of the lighthouse on the coastal hills some 270 feet high to the east of the town.

It is on the section of line down to Cromer that we enjoy some fine views, our first glimpse of the sea, not forgetting Cromer Lighthouse, and the cliffs and other areas dotted, even smothered, with holiday caravans and gaily coloured tents. The spindly mast visible in the south-west is the West Runton television transmitter, a booster for the Tacolneston television transmitter a few miles south of Norwich.

At Cromer there is a four-minute interval for reversal. The driver, confronted by the buffer stops, vacates his cab and strolls to the other end ready to take us the remaining three and three-quarter miles to Sheringham – remnant of the once-proud M&GN Railway, which keeps within the national network the town of Sheringham, for many years the domicile of William Marriott, the monarch of the M&GN.

The wayfarer with a discerning eye and intent on exploring Cromer, the 'Gem of the Norfolk Coast', and perhaps scaling the lighthouse hills for the splendid views of the surrounding area – immortalised as 'Poppyland' by Clement Scott, the foremost dramatic critic of the late nineteenth century who devotedly frequented the district – will notice as he wanders from the platform the initials E&MR wrought in the ironwork of the spandrels of the canopy pillars, a reminder of the Eastern & Midlands Railway which opened the station in 1887.

Inscribed in the ironwork above the entrance to the former booking-hall will be seen the monogram of the old M&GN Railway which in 1893 absorbed the earlier railway and, escaping the 1923 amalgamations, retained its separate identity until the unification of the railways in 1948. Most of the station buildings are occupied by a firm of timber and builders' merchants.

Cromer, like North Walsham, is noted for a man who distinguished himself at sea, though in a very different role: Henry Blogg was for fifty-three years a lifeboatman and served thirty-eight of them as coxswain. In North Lodge Park is a bronze bust of Blogg gazing out over the sea upon which during those many years close on 900 lives were saved by the Cromer lifeboat, its heroic history commemorated in a museum situated on the promenade below.

Resuming our journey we retrace our steps for half a mile as we head due west, the Norwich line curving away on our left. Gathering speed we hurry over a three-arch viaduct spanning a picturesque valley and the village of East Runton nestling below, which, together with West Runton a mile distant, comprises the parish of Runton.

A short distance away on our left and roughly parallel is another viaduct, one of five arches and considerably higher. This formerly carried a short line avoiding Cromer, and enabled such famous seasonal trains as the 'Norfolk Coast Express' and the 'Eastern Belle' – the latter an all-Pullman-car excursion train resplendent in its two-tone livery of cream and umber, lined out in gold – to run direct between London's Liverpool Street Station and Sheringham.

Darting from under a bridge, we hasten alongside the nine-hole (formerly eighteen-hole) West Runton golf-links fringed with hills covered in bracken and gorse, while on our right we gain a clear view of the sea and, in between, the Cromer to Sheringham road dotted with cars, some of them running neck and neck with us. Almost hidden in a dip is West Runton Station, a wooden cabin-like structure in marked contrast to the well-appointed hotel astride the entrance to the links, little more than a stone's throw away.

The bridge under which we now pass, just beyond the concave platform, carries the road to the Roman Camp, a renowned beauty-spot a mile to the south up through wooded country enriched with rhododendrons, and well worth a visit for the panoramic views amid heather and bracken before a backcloth of varying shades of marine blue. The Roman Camp – its connection with the Roman occupation much in doubt – some 300 feet above sea-level, has been in the care of the National Trust since 1924. Teas and refreshments are obtainable here.

Emerging from a wooded cutting we notice on our right Beeston Regis Church not far distant from the edge of the cliff. The church is expected to fall down on to the beach about the year 2129 because of the unremitting encroachments of the sea – a perennial problem along this coast of glacial cliffs formed of loose and incoherent material.

Then, into view on the left, come the tree-encircled ruins of Beeston Priory, a religious house dating back to the reign of King John in the thirteenth century. Tradition has it that a tunnel connects the two edifices separated as they are by a mere half mile. In fact, a few years before the Second World War, some alterations being made in the adjacent Priory Farm led to the discovery of an entrance, which was bricked up.

Also on the left, as the train slackens speed, can be seen Beeston Common, and, just beyond the coast road separating the two, Beeston Bog; the latter, golden in spring and summer with buttercups and gorse, is a naturalist's paradise where such plants as orchids and the elegant grass of Parnassus are to be found, while newts and frogs abound. The site has been designated by the Nature Conservancy Council as one of Special Scientific Interest.

At the same time, looming up on the right with its back to the cliff edge is Beeston Hill, or Hump, though less prominent than of yore due to coastal erosion. From the top a magnificent view of Sheringham and its hilly hinterland, and of the coastline, is the reward for those prepared to make the steep ascent.

Spreading out before us now, on both sides of an embankment, is Sheringham, and after crossing a couple of bridges and passing on our left the red-brick Roman Catholic Church of St Joseph designed by Sir Giles Gilbert Scott, we come gently to a halt at a short wooden asphalted platform which today serves as the Sheringham railhead, thirty and a half miles from Norwich.

NORTH NORFOLK RAILWAY

Alighting from the British Rail train at Sheringham we see, just ahead across Station Road, which once had a level crossing and signal-box, the original station, its buildings on the north platform still in being and now the headquarters of the North Norfolk Railway. The line from Sheringham to Melton Constable was closed in 1964, and part of it was subsequently bought and reopened as a preserved line. The car park adjacent to the station was once an extensive goods yard and from here, for some years before and after the Second World War, flints gathered from the beach were dispatched to Stoke-on-Trent for use in the manufacture of pottery.

From the station, between Easter and the end of September, and at certain other times, a steam and diesel service is operated by the North Norfolk Railway to Weybourne Station, two and three-quarter miles distant. The line is being extended towards Holt, and already a short section of the extension, to Kelling Camp, is open. A timetable for the North Norfolk Railway, also indicating the dates on which it operates, is obtainable from Sheringham Station (telephone 822045).

Trains steam slowly out, past the golf-links, and then climb steadily through undulating fields, over the main coast road, with good views of the wooded hills to the south and the sea to the north. Weybourne Station, situated in a sylvan setting, is roughly a mile inland from the coastal village where there is deep water and where our ancestors, the Angles, are believed to have made their first landing.

The establishment at Weybourne in 1935 of an anti-aircraft practice camp brought much additional traffic to this station, which continued until the camp's abandonment fourteen years after the war ended. In recent years the Sheringham–Weybourne stretch of line has figured in a number of television productions: *Dad's Army*, *Hi-di-Hi*, *'Allo, 'Allo*, *Swallows and Amazons*, *Fall of Eagles* and D. H. Lawrence's famous novel *Sons and Lovers* to mention just some of them.

The halt at Kelling Camp, three-quarters of a mile west of Weybourne, was opened in the summer of 1984 and the track is now being extended to another halt, at Kelling Aviaries. A further advance, to the Holt Road, is the aim of the North Norfolk Railway.

This railway can also figure in the plans of walkers in this area. For instance, half a mile south of Sheringham is the beauty-spot, Pretty Corner, set high in a heathery hinterland – at 327 feet one of the highest points in Norfolk – and very rewarding for the rambler. Westwards one can follow the cliff and golf-links almost into the village of Weybourne and then, turning inland along a track to strike the coast road by the inhabited five-storey tower windmill, make for the station and journey back to Sheringham by steam train.

Holt, which the North Norfolk Railway ultimately hopes to reach, is a pleasant Georgian town some six miles inland from Sheringham. Just before entering the town aboard one of the privately operated buses at present plying between Sheringham and Holt, one passes Gresham's School (1555), where were educated two twentieth-century celebrities: the poet and dramatist W. H. Auden and the Lowestoft-born composer, Benjamin Britten, OM, who was ennobled shortly before his death.

Class J15 0–6–0 No. 7564 arrives at Weybourne Station. (*Photo:* Brian Fisher)

Restored Diesel Railbus No. E79960 (with No. 79963 coupled behind) at Weybourne Station. (*Photo:* Brian Fisher)

WHERRY LINE

by Trevor Garrod

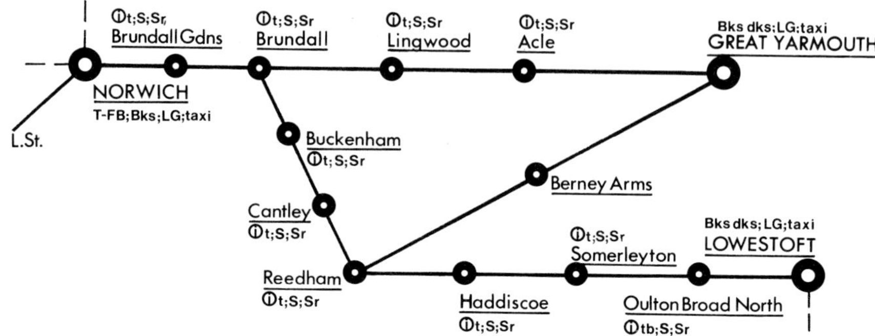

The wherry was a wooden barge whose large sail moved slowly across the flat East Norfolk landscape as it bore its cargoes along the winding Waveney, Yare, and Bure, down the smaller rivers and across the main Broads.

Trading wherries are long since gone, and apart from a very few cargo vessels to Norwich, the rivers and lakes are now the preserve of cruisers, yachts, and other pleasure craft.

The name of the wherry lives on in British Rail's group of lines between Norwich, Great Yarmouth, and Lowestoft, over which diesel railcars provide a fast and frequent service – never far from water, serving several riverside communities *en route*.

On leaving Norwich, Wherry line trains are soon speeding along the left bank of the Yare, an old branch of which skirts Thorpe village, backed by luxuriant rising woodland, just to the north.

Five miles along the line is Brundall, a growing commuter village with a station and also a halt (Brundall Gardens) built in 1924. The train runs through woodland with glints of water on either side, past boatyards, a large pub and, a short walk from the station, the River Yare among beds of reed, alder, and willow. In summer, it is possible to enjoy a leisurely ride by pleasure boat between Foundry Bridge (by the entrance to Norwich Station) and Brundall.

A pleasant run through alders and willows, with Strumpshaw Fen Bird Reserve on the right, brings us to the isolated station of Buckenham, seven and three-quarter miles from Norwich, with an octagonal church tower peering over rising land to the left.

Now the Yare Valley marshes open out, the river winding between dikes to the south of us, interrupted only by Cantley dominated by the impressive silos of its sugar-beet factory, from which dense white smoke billows during the autumn campaign.

Reedham Ferry – the only crossing for road vehicles between Norwich and Great Yarmouth – can be seen to the south as we pull into the station serving the large riverside village. At Reedham, Great Yarmouth trains take a single track straight across the marshes, sometimes pausing on the way at the other station in the parish of Reedham – Berney Arms.

Berney Arms is unique – a riverside pub, one or two isolated farms, and a massive

Train passing Berney Arms Mill. (*Photo:* R. C. Vincent)

windmill in the middle of flat pastureland, with no road access but instead, a tiny windswept platform. Once a week, a postman comes out by train from Great Yarmouth to deliver mail. Some trains only stop when required. Berney Arms Mill is open from April to the end of September.

The fifteen-minute run from Reedham to Great Yarmouth also provides the best view of Halvergate Marshes, currently the subject of controversy over their proposed draining.

Soon the train is rounding the northern edge of Breydon Water with its varied wildlife. On rising land to the south can be seen the low stone walls of Burgh Castle – the Roman fort of Garianonum built to defend what was then a great estuary from Saxon marauders.

Some twenty and a half miles from Norwich, the train runs past sidings and enters the curving platforms of Vauxhall Station – the only survivor of Great Yarmouth's three stations, damaged in the Second World War and largely rebuilt in 1960. Freight facilities were withdrawn from the adjacent yard in 1984; while previously in 1976 the rail line which crossed the River Bure, at the station approach, and gave direct access to the main quay, was also closed.

Great Yarmouth remains a busy port, but all freight must currently go by road, and a by-pass with a new road bridge over the mouth of Breydon Water is currently being built. Most visitors to the town are, however, likely to head across the River Bure to find themselves within a few minutes in the extensive market-place with the stately Church of St Nicholas at one end and the Market Gates Shopping Centre at the other. The museums and remains of medieval walls are a less-well-known aspect of this town which most people will know as one of the leading resorts of the East Coast. With neighbouring Gorleston it boasts six miles of sandy beaches, and the central Golden Mile, with the greatest concentration of holiday attractions, is some fifteen minutes' walk from the station.

The Lowestoft trains rattle over Reedham Swing Bridge (with good views of the waterfront), then bear left to run alongside the New Cut – a two-and-a-half-mile canal cut straight as a die from the Yare to the Waveney in 1833, to enable cargo vessels to reach Norwich by way of Lowestoft rather than Great Yarmouth. The two coastal towns have long been rivals.

In fact, the Norwich–Lowestoft Navigation had a brief heyday – partly because the Great Yarmouth Port and Haven Commissioners undertook works to improve their own passage to Norwich; and partly because of the building of this railway in 1847. The New Cut is, therefore, nowadays used purely by pleasure craft.

Just before Haddiscoe, the train passes under a concrete road bridge built across the line and the New Cut in 1960. Haddiscoe Station is over a mile and a half from the village of that name, but rather closer to St Olaves, a hamlet on the opposite bank of the Waveney, set among trees. Legend has it that the Viking Olaf (Olave) and his longboat haunt the river in these parts. There is a pleasant riverside pub in St Olaves and a ruined priory (entry free). A mile farther east is Fritton with a church of Saxon origin and a long serpentine lake in woodland, with a country park open to the public in summer.

Indeed, there is much of interest in Lothingland, this northern tip of Suffolk (some of whose parishes were transferred to Norfolk in 1974) – the churches of Ashby and Lound, Somerleyton Hall and Gardens, Burgh Castle, Blundeston with its Dickensian associations. It is good cycling country, and Haddiscoe or Somerleyton stations are ideal railheads from which to explore it.

The train passes the earthworks of the former Beccles–Great Yarmouth line at Haddiscoe (which was once an interchange on two levels) and follows the curves of the Waveney to Somerleyton, a picturesque station designed to please the Lord of the Manor and now being restored. The railway gives a better view of the restored Herringfleet Mill than any road can. These marshes were once peppered with such pumping mills.

The Wherry line is now in Suffolk and soon gives views of Oulton Church – the 'Marshland Sentinel' – with its unusual central tower, on rising land to the left; while opposite, on the Norfolk side of the Waveney, is the Church of Burgh St Peter, with its curious five-stage bell-tower, nestling in trees on the river bank.

A quick run through leafy suburbs brings our train to Oulton Broad North, conveniently situated for the nearby lake with its park, swimming-pool, and other attractions, including Bank Holiday fêtes and speed-boat racing in summer. We then follow the same route as the East Suffolk line trains into Lowestoft, where we can smell the salt air as we alight at the station, the most easterly on British Rail. A mere stone's throw away is the harbour with its trawlers, and two minutes' walk over the bascule bridge is the sandy beach. Outside the station, a statue, *The Call of the Sea*, actually points the way along the town's pedestrianised main shopping street, towards the rival resort of Great Yarmouth.

An alternative rail route to Great Yarmouth leaves the main line at Brundall and heads for Lingwood – which the sailing wherries never reached. Wherry line trains serve this growing commuter village on the direct Brundall–Great Yarmouth line opened in 1883, and continue through undulating wheat fields dotted with typical Norfolk round-towered churches to Acle – a large village with a well-known cattle market – before striking out across the marshes, parallel to the A47 to join the older route from Reedham on the shores of Breydon Water.

EAST SUFFOLK LINE

by Louis Hipperson

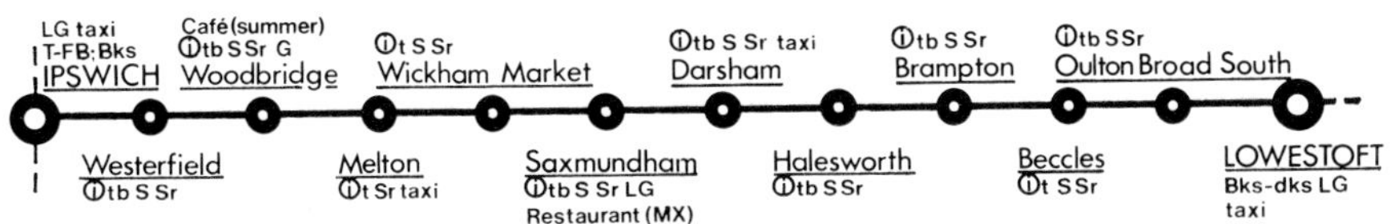

This line (opened throughout in 1859) runs from Ipswich, Suffolk's county town, to Lowestoft, in the north-east of the county and its second town in size. Much of the seaward side of Suffolk is served, including several small towns, of considerable historic and other interest.

When the present edition of this book was being prepared, the line was still in the process of being modernised so as to reduce running and maintenance costs. Work started in 1982 and should be completed by the end of 1985.

From Ipswich to Beccles, on the Norfolk border, the line forms an approximate demarcation between two of Suffolk's geographical regions. Between the railway and the coast are the Sandlings, once almost completely covered with heaths, grazed by large flocks of sheep. The heaths are now much diminished and the sheep have vanished. The light soil is increasingly being brought under the plough or afforested. West of the railway lies so-called High Suffolk, a low plateau, from whence many rivers and streams flow into the North Sea. The railway, therefore, crosses a large number of valleys of varying character. As no viaducts or high embankments were built to carry the line, it has, by railway standards, a surprising total of quite steep gradients. This may seem strange to those who imagine that all East Anglia is as flat as a pancake. The physical geography, together with the many small woods and isolated trees still, in general, existing in the neighbourhood of the line, produce scenery that, while not spectacular, is very pleasant.

The directions 'right' and 'left' in the following description of a journey along the line are based on the assumption that the reader is seated facing towards the front of the train. Figures in parentheses after the name of a station indicate its mileage from Ipswich.

Within a mile of leaving Ipswich, the train diverges from the main Norwich line at East Suffolk Junction. The route as far as Westerfield ($3\frac{1}{2}$), the first station, is described in the article on the Felixstowe branch. Beyond Westerfield, the train, now travelling almost due east, passes through a succession of cuttings above the River Fynn (or Finn), a little to the north. An automated, open level crossing marks the site of Bealings Station ($7\frac{1}{4}$), whose passenger service was withdrawn in 1956. Two minutes later we cross the Fynn and almost at once a bridge over the A12 (the main London–Great Yarmouth road) noting on the left the commencement of Woodbridge By-pass and on the right Martlesham Creek. The Fynn flows into the Creek, an inlet of the River Deben. Next come extensive nurseries on each side.

The line curves north-east to reveal a general view of the town of Woodbridge on the left. Opposite, close at hand, is the estuary of the Deben, backed by rising partly wooded countryside. Between rail and river is a delightful promenade, with model-yacht pond and bandstand. We see a large number of yachts, cruisers, and other pleasure craft of all types. Woodbridge Station ($10\frac{1}{4}$) is a stone's throw from the

A 4-car DMU train packed with summer holidaymakers returning from Lowestoft leaves Woodbridge for Ipswich. (*Photo:* J. A. Howie)

water's edge. Near by are an eighteenth-century tide-mill (open to visitors on Bank Holidays and from June to October, but check days and times) and a modern swimming-pool.

Apart from its aquatic interest, Woodbridge is one of the most attractive towns in Suffolk. It has the fine fifteenth-century Parish Church of St Mary, a small museum, many beautiful old buildings, a public school, an abundance of hotels, pubs and eating-places, and an excellent range of shops.

The bus station is only a few minutes' walk from the railway station. On leaving the station exit, immediately bear right in front of Station House (now a guest-house and café) and make towards a cinema, at the entrance to which turn half-right into Quayside. Continue forward as far as the factory of Turban Foods Ltd. Here turn left into the Turban Centre, where the bus station forms part of a complex that includes a well-designed small shopping precinct, with access to Woodbridge's main street. Eastern Counties buses run to Framlingham (infrequent service, none on Sundays), another attractive town, with a ruined twelfth-century castle (mainly curtain-walls and towers), a Late Perpendicular church (notable tombs, some with effigies) and Framlingham College, the Suffolk county memorial to the Prince Consort; and to Wickham Market (about hourly weekdays, few on Sundays), a quiet little town, its most noticeable feature the lofty spire of its church which is unusual in Suffolk. Belle Coaches provide a sparse service to the village of Orford (essential to obtain details in advance of travel), a quaint, decayed pocket borough

close to the coast – see the partly ruined church and Norman polygonal castle keep and eat locally bred oysters.

Our train continues through Melton, a northern suburb of Woodbridge. Melton Station ($11\frac{1}{2}$) had its passenger service restored from 3 September 1984, after being without one since 1955. Next to the station is Melton Riverside Amenity Site, offering, despite its prosaic name, an inviting, small nature reserve that includes a picnic site. Woodbridge–Orford buses pass the station; alternatively, Orford is but an hour's cycle ride away. Trips on cycle or on foot can also be made into Rendlesham Forest and the heaths that still remain between the Deben and the sea. Within two miles lies the site of the famous Sutton Hoo seventh-century ship burial, discovered in 1939. Archaeologists are divided in opinion as to the purpose of the burial. Some consider that it was probably a cenotaph in honour of an East Anglian King of the Wuffinga dynasty, as yet inconclusively identified; others say that the vessel served as his tomb. The priceless treasures found in the ship are now in the British Museum, although replicas exist in Ipswich Museum and a permanent Sutton Hoo exhibition is in Woodbridge Museum.

We keep to the Deben Valley after Melton, but the river is now much reduced in width and ceases to be navigable. Within a distance of three miles, we cross the river as many times.

Wickham Market ($15\frac{3}{4}$) is actually in the village of Campsea Ashe (or Campsey Ash), two miles from the town after which it is named. No public transport links station and town. From this station, branch-line passenger trains ran to Framlingham until 1952, but the rails have been lifted, leaving few vestiges of the route.

Just beyond the station, on the right, is a close view of the village church, its tower crowned by a spirelet. Soon we go through a double line of electricity pylons, leading to the nuclear power station at Sizewell, on the coast, and descend to follow for a short distance the valley of a tributary of the River Alde. Crossing the main river, we can look over the marshes on the right to the distant Snape Maltings, now of concert fame but served until 1960 by a freight-only branch, traces of which are difficult to discern.

Three miles farther on, we drop down to the compact little town of Saxmundham, nestling in the valley of the Fromus, another tributary of the Alde. Prominent on the left as we approach the town are a large water-tower and a school. The station ($22\frac{1}{2}$) is the railhead for Leiston and Aldeburgh, both larger than Saxmundham, and the twentieth-century planned village of Thorpeness. Buses from Saxmundham run to Leiston and Aldeburgh about every hour (two only on Sundays), but few go to Thorpeness. Some of these buses call at the station forecourt; otherwise they must be boarded at the bus station, situated in High Street next to the modern post office and telephone exchange and reached on foot in five minutes by descending to the T-junction and turning left. Leiston was only a village until the nineteenth-century development of its ironworks, founded in 1778 but closed down completely in recent years and many of its buildings demolished, a notable exception being the Long Shop, a regional industrial museum (open Wednesdays, May–September, admission free). Aldeburgh, a coastal resort, is internationally famous for its annual music festival, linked with the late Benjamin Britten, the Lowestoft-born composer.

A short climb from Saxmundham brings us to the junction with the single-track branch line (right) used for taking waste from the nuclear power station at Sizewell. Until 1966, this line, which now ends on the eastern outskirts of Leiston, carried a passenger service to that town, Thorpeness and Aldeburgh. Soon, on the left, and in the near distance, we see the straggling village of Kelsale, its church tower standing out.

The next station, Darsham ($26\frac{3}{4}$), entered by a level crossing over the A12, is some way from the main part of that village and one and a half miles from the larger village of Yoxford, on the Minsmere River (or Yox) and known as 'the Garden of Suffolk'. The walker who alights at Darsham, as at other stations on the line, can visit the Suffolk Heritage coast, with its long-distance footpath. Darsham is the most convenient station for the cyclist or walker who wishes to explore the varied countryside surrounding the villages of Westleton and Dunwich, the latter probably the outstanding example in Britain of a large historic town and seaport almost completely lost through cliff erosion.

Having descended to Darsham, we rise again to go through a series of cuttings parallel to the road through the village of Bramfield (right), where it is sometimes possible to catch a brief sight of the church's detached round tower. As soon as we clear the cuttings, we cross the road on the level and in a few seconds we can see it curving away to the left into the town of Halesworth, the modern development of which is visible – it has doubled in size since the Second World War. The train now goes down one of the steepest gradients on the line into the valley of the River Blyth. About a mile away, half-right, the restored wooden post-mill, painted white, at Holton takes the eye.

As the train enters Halesworth Station (32) over a bridge above the Southwold road, watch out for the abutments of another bridge immediately on the right, a

River Deben at Woodbridge.

Snape Maltings.

June 1983, the 14.58 Ipswich–Lowestoft train pauses at Saxmundham Station while passengers await the arrival of the 14.50 Lowestoft–Ipswich. (*Photo:* Howard Quayle)

remnant of the single-track narrow-gauge railway that ran from Halesworth to Southwold (1879–1929). Halesworth has a large church, with double aisles on each side, many other interesting buildings, and a town park that merits a visit.

Fairly close to the station are bus stops, one for Bungay and the other for Southwold. For the former, cross the road on leaving the station on the down side to follow a footpath that runs alongside the railway. On reaching another road (Norwich Road), turn right over a bridge and the bus stop will be found on the left after a short distance. The stop for Southwold is outside the United Reformed Church in Quay Street. Again, leave the station on the down side, but turn left downhill to a T-junction, with a public house on the left-hand corner. Here turn right and the stop is a few yards along on the right. Southwold is noted for its unspoilt (almost Victorian) character, magnificent church, lighthouse, and breezy common; while Bungay has yet another castle, two medieval churches, a butter cross, and a very large common in a loop of the River Waveney. Those who wish to explore Halesworth may find it more convenient to catch a bus from the bus stand at Steeple End, adjoining the far side of the churchyard and reached by following the Ipswich direction signs through the town.

From Halesworth Station, the train makes a long ascent, passing, at a level crossing within the first half mile, the site of the terminal station of the Halesworth, Beccles & Haddiscoe Railway (opened 1854), the nucleus of the East Suffolk line. Over a mile from the present Halesworth Station, we pass under a road bridge and then the gradient eases. To the right, the landscape is not improved by the large number of unsightly buildings, on a former airfield, and now used by a very well-known firm of turkey farmers.

The train descends – this must now seem a statutory obligation on the approach to stops! – to Brampton Station (36), well over two miles from the village of that name, but, soon, much nearer on the left, we see the scattered small village of

Redisham, where the late Adrian Bell, the renowned writer on country matters, lived at the Old Vicarage for some years.

Three miles beyond Brampton, we reach the top of a long descent, Beccles Bank, down which we speed to reach Beccles Station (40½), formerly the most important intermediate one on the line and, up to 1959, a junction. In that year the Beccles–Great Yarmouth (Southtown) section of the East Suffolk line was closed to passengers. The line from Beccles via Bungay to Tivetshall (on the main Ipswich–Norwich line) had been similarly closed in 1953. Both lines have now been lifted, although infrequent buses run from Beccles to Great Yarmouth and Bungay. The bus station, in Old Market, is under ten minutes' walk from the railway station. Follow Station Road towards the town centre and, after the traffic lights, take the first turn right (Smallgate).

Beccles Parish Church of St Michael is of noble proportions. It has a massive stone-faced, detached tower (visible from the train) and a beautifully carved stone south porch. The town is a well-known Broadland centre, being situated on the River Waveney, here the boundary between Norfolk and Suffolk. From the station, we can see (left) the extensive works of the eminent printers, William Clowes.

Just beyond the station platforms, watch out for the former small engine-shed (left). The line is now bearing gradually to the east. The level crossing over the Beccles By-pass indicates the site of the junction with the Great Yarmouth line, whose course can be traced bearing slightly left. We traverse several miles of marshes, but the scenery is not monotonous, owing to the woods on either side. At one point, the train runs for about half a mile close to the main Beccles–Lowestoft road – and overtakes all traffic!

Oulton Broad South Station (46¾) lies in a large western suburb of Lowestoft. Soon we cross a swing bridge over Lake Lothing, a wide sheet of water that stretches away on our right to reach the harbour at Lowestoft; while to our left, on the other side of a nearby road bridge, is another expanse of water, Oulton Broad, usually a hive of activity. A few hundred yards farther on, we pass the ends of the platforms at Oulton Broad North Station (left) and join the Norwich–Lowestoft route to finish our journey at Lowestoft Station (49).

Oulton Broad.

FELIXSTOWE BRANCH

by Howard Quayle

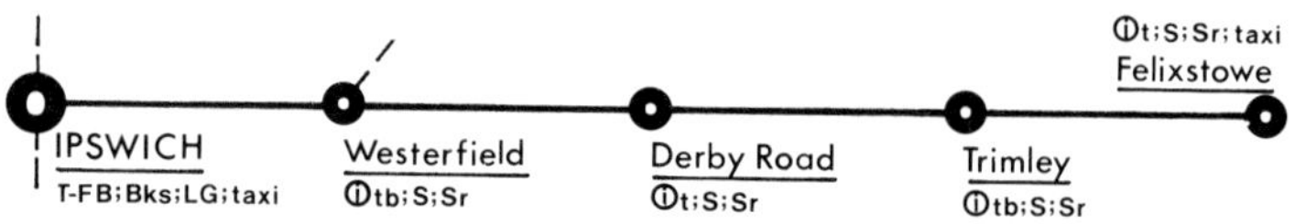

This line remains the only 'classic' East Anglian branch line never to have been proposed for closure, and the reasons why are not hard to see – healthy all-year-round commuter traffic, enhanced by holiday-makers during the summer, and with a still expanding base of Freightliner traffic from the port of Felixstowe.

The line's route out of Ipswich is unusual, since it virtually doubles back on itself to reach the town's eastern suburbs, one and a half miles away as the crow flies, but six miles distant for the rail traveller! One reason for this is the use, by Felixstowe trains, of the 'main' East Suffolk line as far as Westerfield, reached after a steep climb of 1 in 90/150 across high embankments and through deep cuttings. Westerfield Station (three and a half miles from Ipswich) presents a rather dismal sight, with its 'bus stop' shelters, although, on the right, wooden buildings erected in 1877 by the Felixstowe Railway & Pier Co. still survive. With the picturesque village of Westerfield on the left, the train clatters across the junction on to a single line, climbing away steeply southwards at 1 in 85.

The diesel multiple unit has been running through the countryside since before Westerfield and the unwary find it strange to plunge back once more into suburban Ipswich, the line having completed its arc from Ipswich Station. Once across Spring Road Viaduct – the line's major engineering work with a fine but fleeting view of the town to the right – the train enters the loop at Derby Road Station (six miles from Ipswich), where the sidings handle both coal and scrap-metal traffic.

The single line now leaves Ipswich for the second time, and with the Suffolk Showground on the left, plunges into the forest area around the exclusive village of Nacton; here a single-span bridge, completed in 1982, carries the branch over its major competitor, the dual-carriageway A45. Beyond the bridge lie the remains of Orwell Station, closed in 1959 when the line was dieselised and services accelerated.

Emerging from the Scottish-type scenery of the pine forest, the train, now running along virtually dead-level track, passes the rurally situated head office of Norsk-Hydro (formerly Fisons) Fertilisers on the right. The outlines of villages are prominent in the flat landscape, as are the tall buildings of the British Telecom Research Centre, away to the east at Martlesham. To the west, however, come views of coastal Suffolk, glimpses of the Orwell Estuary being followed by vistas of the modern port of Felixstowe.

Once through the loop at Trimley Station (fourteen miles from Ipswich), where tokens are exchanged for the last time, the view of Felixstowe Docks, close at hand, contrasts with the medieval town of Harwich, on the other side of the Stour – particularly dominant are St Nicholas Church and the pagoda-inspired lighthouse, one of the earliest in Britain. Just beyond Trimley Station, a new branch line, about one and a half miles long and running due south, is planned, in order to provide more convenient access to the port's North Freightliner Terminal, opened in 1983.

Speed is now down to 20 mph as the line curves into the cutting at Felixstowe Beach Junction, the freight-only dock line diverging to the right, and a minute later, the train comes to a halt in the single-platformed Felixstowe Station (fifteen and three-quarter miles from Ipswich).

The main part of the town's station – built in 1898 during its Late Victorian heyday as a fashionable resort – is being converted into a shopping centre: the developer has already restored the principal buildings, and plans to have a 'railway theme' running throughout the whole complex. From the station, passengers can walk straight down Hamilton Road – a pleasant thoroughfare with some shops still retaining their Victorian façades – to the seafront.

Although, for many, the latter may have the more obvious attraction, the town itself, which grew up in the late nineteenth century at the top of the hill above the promenade, is well worth a close look. Because of its rapid growth between 1881 and 1891, the architectural style displays a homogeneity not often found elsewhere, although the observant visitor may notice, intermingled with solid Victorian red-brick, the flamboyant designs of T. W. Cotman, a noted local architect: his crowning triumph was undoubtedly the Neo-Jacobean Felix Hotel in Cobbold Road, dating from 1903, which is now undergoing conversion into luxury flats.

The seafront at the foot of the low cliffs has all the attractions found in larger resorts: pier, funfair, cafés and restaurants, and invigorating sea breezes. Safe beaches, coupled with the attractions of the busy shipping lanes offshore, make Felixstowe a very pleasant place in which to spend a few hours.

Finally, ramblers and nature-lovers may note that Felixstowe is the southern terminus of the fifty-mile Suffolk Coast Path to Lowestoft, for which Suffolk County Council has produced an attractive brochure.

MANNINGTREE – HARWICH

by John Hull

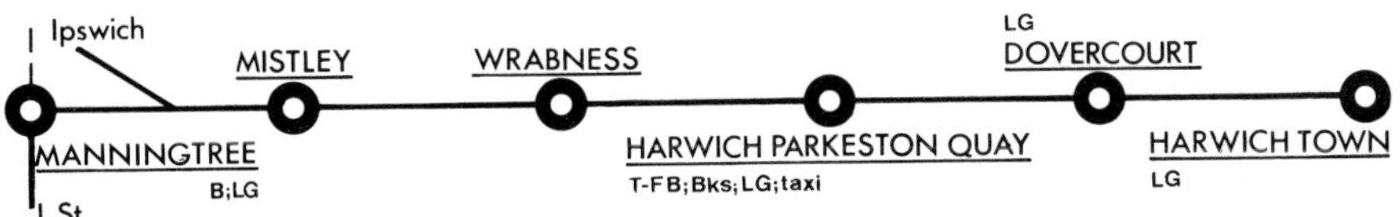

Opened in 1854, the line from Manningtree to Harwich is really two completely different railways; on the one hand it is a fairly typical branch line, departing from a bay platform at a junction station and proceeding in leisurely fashion through a succession of small stations to a terminus in a moderately sized coastal town. On the other hand, it is a busy double-track main line carrying heavy freight and passenger traffic from all over the country to one of its major ports.

The best way to see the line's two faces is to board the two-car local train at Manningtree, a station with two claims to fame: being the windiest and the one with most 'real ales' on sale. From here, the train immediately leaves the main line, curving eastwards to climb out of, but never leave, the valley of the River Stour. The train window affords magnificent views across the water to the Suffolk side some mile or more away.

Passing through Manningtree in a steeply graded cutting, our train reaches open

Electric trains like this one on the Braintree branch will soon be running to Harwich. (*Photo:* John C. Baker)

countryside just before its first stop at Mistley, probably the best example of a wayside station left in East Anglia. Here is an intact goods yard, a staffed station with a proper booking-office and waiting-room, and even a branch which slopes steeply down to the quay with a reversal *en route*. The station is surrounded by maltings, some traditional and one very modern.

From Mistley the train soon emerges on to a high embankment, with views northwards to the Royal Hospital School at Holbrook. Speed rises as the remains of Bradfield Station (closed in 1956) are passed, followed quickly by the remnants of Priory Halt, a platform built to serve the Royal Naval Mine Depot, now closed. Wrabness soon comes into view, another delightful station serving an isolated village. From here it is only a twenty-minute walk to a very pleasant river beach on the banks of the Stour.

For the next two miles, the train runs through woodland, mostly chestnut, which until recently was used commercially for fencing. In the autumn the varying colours make a most impressive sight, particularly to the north with the river as a backdrop. Then, suddenly, the real reason for the line's present existence comes into view, as the train drops from the higher valley side and turns on to the marshes. Originally, it would have continued in a straight line, but when the Great Eastern Railway fell out with Harwich Borough in the 1870s, it decided to build a new port on the marshy Ray Island, just outside the Corporation's boundary. Hence the creation of Parkeston Quay, opened in 1883 and named after the then Chairman of the company.

The port itself has been totally rebuilt in the past fifteen years to cater for modern traffic developments. It remains very busy, even though road traffic now intrudes on what was once solely a rail port – much to the annoyance of local residents.

Running through the freight yards, the large passenger ferries may be seen to the north, and our train, now seeming very small in the long platforms of Parkeston Quay Station, crosses to the up platform, for the remainder of the journey is single track as far as passenger trains are concerned.

Leaving the station, the train swings back off the marshes towards the original line, passing the container terminal on the left and masses of cars for import or export on the right. Here the double track still exists, but the old down line is now used as a very long siding for freight trains. Passing mudflats, we enter Dovercourt Station, until recently having the suffix 'Bay' to denote the seaside attractions of the town. This is, to local people at least, the most important station on the line. It is then only a short ride to the passenger terminus at Harwich Town, where only one of the three platforms is used for its original purpose, the others being used to unload the car-carrying trains which make up a large proportion of the line's traffic. Even this is not quite the end of the line, for a short branch leads off northwards to the train ferry berth a few hundred yards away. There is also a passenger ferry across the estuary to Felixstowe.

It has been suggested on many occasions that the Harwich branch is one of the most interesting lines still in use, both from the railway and scenic angles. Its importance is also such that, by May 1986, it will be operated by electric trains.

COLCHESTER–CLACTON/WALTON

by Tony Baxter

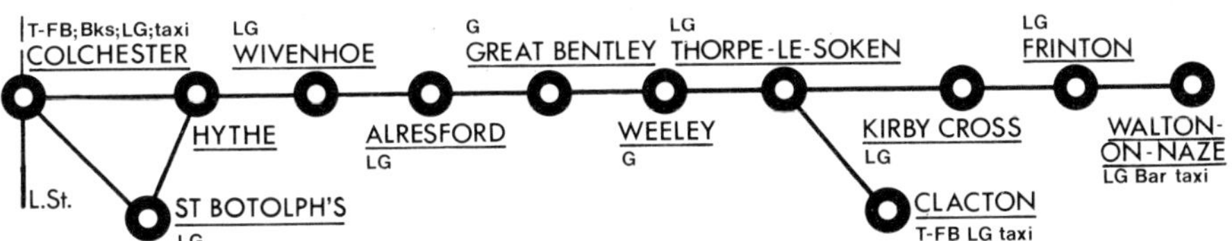

Low rainfall and long hours of sunshine coupled with excellent beaches have made the coastline of north-east Essex a popular holiday area. Walton had already begun to develop as a resort by the time that the Eastern Counties Railway reached Colchester from London in 1843. The opening in 1863 of the Tendring Hundred Railway from Colchester to Walton boosted its popularity and led to the development of neighbouring Frinton and Clacton later in the nineteenth century.

Leaving Colchester, our route diverges from the main line to Norwich a short distance from the North Station and winds its way through the eastern outskirts of the town, giving glimpses of timber-framed buildings to act as a reminder of Colchester's historic past. At Eastgate the line to the coast forms a triangular junction with the short branch to St Botolph's Station, served only by local trains but very conveniently situated in relation to the shopping centre and bus station. There are buses to such rail-less places as Mersea Island (hourly) and (less frequently) to Tollesbury. Here may be seen a section of the town walls dating from the third century and nearby are the remains of St Botolph's Priory. The branch was also constructed to serve the Colchester garrison but an extension to the barracks, although authorised, was never built.

Returning to the main line to the coast, the train follows the north bank of the River Colne, past Colchester's Hythe Docks, the highest point reached by ocean-going vessels. The towers of the University of Essex may be seen on somewhat higher ground shortly before arriving at Wivenhoe. Here the station booking-office still boasts a cast-iron fireplace incorporating the coat of arms of the Great Eastern Railway. Immediately opposite the station entrance a footpath leads down to the river where once a ferry plied across to Rowhedge on the opposite bank; now a six-mile detour by road is necessary. Wivenhoe declined in importance as a port with the deepening of the river to the Hythe in 1854, although some shipbuilding still remains; now, however, it is a very popular yachting centre. Interesting walks may be taken along the river, both upstream towards the university and downstream toward Alresford Creek. Many species of bird life may be seen including heron and kingfisher, while large flocks of swans live in the vicinity.

Continuing our journey from Wivenhoe, we pass the trackbed of the Brightlingsea branch (closed 1963) as the train climbs out of the river valley. This is fruit-farming country and vast orchards may be seen on either side of the line. Approaching Great Bentley, the twelfth-century church is clearly visible on the left although the tower was not added until the fourteenth century. The station is one of the best kept on the line with a sunken ornamental garden surrounded by flower-beds and inhabited by gnomes.

The first indication that we are approaching a holiday area comes as we pass the caravan site at Weeley set in pleasant woodland. Shortly after, as the train slows for the Thorpe-le-Soken Stop, a flying-saucer-like structure is just visible on the skyline to the right of the track: it is in fact an air-traffic-control beacon, an aid to aircraft navigation.

Thorpe-le-Soken is a busy junction station located a mile from the village it purports to serve. When trains first ran in 1867, the line continued only to Walton, but in 1882 a single-track branch to Clacton was opened. Clacton gained rapidly in popularity in the early days of this century and the line was doubled soon after the opening of Butlin's Holiday Camp. Now Butlin's has closed, the line is due to be reduced to single track once more. However, a £2,000,000 electric traction maintenance depot was constructed on a site adjacent to Clacton Station in 1981 for the servicing of the electric multiple-unit stock which makes up all trains in the area. Prior to 1981 some work was carried out in the converted steam locomotive shed while other work had to be carried out at depots elsewhere because of a lack of facilities. From the station, a short walk through the town centre, past the amusement arcades, brings us to the beach with its pier and roller-coaster. From the nearby airfield, pleasure flights may be taken in summer over the surrounding countryside and along the coast towards Harwich and Walton backwaters.

From Thorpe-le-Soken, the Walton train heads northwards along the single line past Kirby Cross, where there is a passing loop, and then, with the sea in view, towards Frinton. The station was opened in 1888 in response to the growing popularity of Frinton as a residential area which has become a select resort with tree-lined avenues and a broad greensward topping low cliffs on the seafront. Continuing towards Walton, the original route of the railway is still visible; in 1929 cliff erosion made it necessary to reconstruct this section farther inland.

At Walton only one of the two original platforms remains in use. The locomotive depot has been converted into a coach park, but the site of the turntable can easily be found. The station is situated on the cliff-top less than a hundred yards from the beach which is the main attraction for the many thousands of visitors who come here every summer. There is also a pier with amusement arcades but the steamers which used to ply along the East Anglian coast, calling at Clacton as well as

Seafront and Pier, Clacton-on-Sea.

Walton, have long since gone. A short walk along the beach and the busy central area gives way to the wide open spaces of the Naze itself, a promontory now, alas, rapidly crumbling into the sea. Here is the Trinity House Tower, built in 1720 to aid navigation and within sight of the ports of Harwich and Felixstowe. Much cross-Channel shipping can be observed; but for many visitors it is the bird life which they have come to see. Hundreds of sand-martins make their homes in the cliffs every summer while many other species of bird may be observed both here and around the neighbouring backwaters. This was the setting Arthur Ransome chose for *Secret Water*, one of his 'Swallows and Amazons' books about a children's yachting holiday. The backwaters are also the home of the Walton and Frinton Yacht Club, one further attraction that brings visitors to this part of the Essex coast every summer.

STOUR VALLEY LINE

by Mike Davies

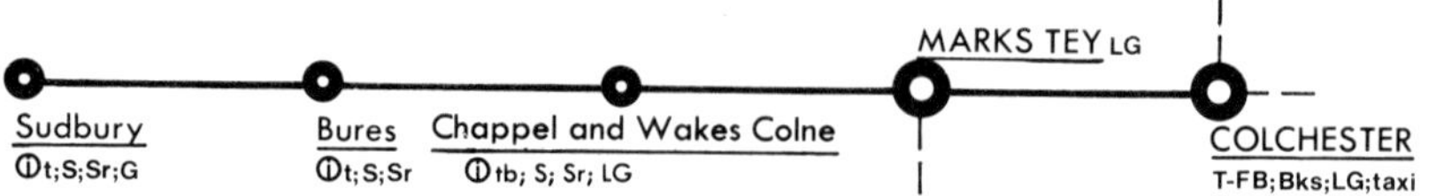

Background

With the coming of railways to East Anglia, the ancient and prosperous market town of Sudbury, the 'Eatanswill' of *The Pickwick Papers* and the birthplace of Thomas Gainsborough, was a natural choice for connection to the burgeoning rail network of Victorian England. The Colchester, Stour Valley & Halstead Railway duly opened to Sudbury with appropriate ceremony on 2 July 1849, reaching Cambridge on 1 June 1865 and Bury St Edmunds on 9 August 1865. The Beeching axe struck in the 1960s, leaving the original Marks Tey–Sudbury line as the truncated survivor of an extensive network of rural lines traversing the Essex–Suffolk border.

The Journey – into the Unknown

On joining the branch train at Marks Tey (reputedly the coldest station in Essex) the traveller will immediately notice that the branch describes a sharp 180 degree curve and in a few minutes the train is bearing away at right angles to the station platform into the delightful rural and heavily wooded Essex uplands. Marks Tey once sported a refreshment room (latterly run by two ancient ladies who religiously locked the door whenever a train arrived!) and a fine Great Eastern station building adjacent to the over-bridge at the north end. Now only a modern booking-office, and a fragment of the once-extensive canopy remain.

The train is soon speeding down the side of the Colne Valley, curving round the line's principal engineering work: Chappel Viaduct, striding across the roofs of the village of the same name. This magnificent structure is 1,066 feet in length, has thirty-two arches and achieves a height of 75 feet above the valley floor. Its construction consumed over 7,000,000 Suffolk White bricks. So we grind to a halt in Chappel and Wakes Colne Station, once a busy junction with the independent (in mind and fact) Colne Valley Railway, a small concern linking Chappel and Haverhill with its own engineering works at Halstead, the headquarters of the line.

Chappel is now home to the Stour Valley Railway Preservation Society, an energetic body of enthusiasts who steam at least one of their collection of vintage locomotives on regular open week-ends throughout the summer. The buildings are being lovingly restored to their former glory by the society. The imposing cast-iron footbridge spanning the tracks was recently rescued from Sudbury Station, and plans are afoot to reconstruct the buildings on the disused platform to the right of the track.

Accelerating out of the station past sidings packed with a veritable Aladdin's Cave of vintage stock on the right, an imposing signal-box and the old station pub (still with its engraved glass windows) on the left, we pass the junction with the Colne Valley Railway immediately beyond the road bridge. A solitary road bridge standing marooned in an orchard to the left bears silent testimony to the passing of a bustling little line. We press on through woods and leafy cuttings that form a green arch overhead in summer, and then as the track dips away we pick up speed and burst out into the Stour Valley, rattling down the side on a 1 in 90 incline which can prove daunting to the return service on a slippery autumn day.

A magnificent vista down the valley to the Vale of Dedham unfolds to the right. The imposing tower of Stoke-by-Nayland Church stands sentinel on the far side of the valley, while to our left, as we rush towards Mount Bures level crossing, stands a wooded mound by the little church, reputedly the burial-place of Boadicea; more recently the site of a fortified manor house.

We descend rapidly into Bures (pronounced Bu-ures), a compact village of great charm and many pubs nestling in the bottom of the valley. On the far side stands a small chapel on St Edmund Hill where, on Christmas Day 855, Edmund Saint and Martyr was crowned King of East Anglia.

The train moves off down the Stour Valley on the final leg of its journey, keeping close company with the river – providing some of the finest fishing in East Anglia, and giving a grandstand view of some of the most attractive countryside of the Essex–Suffolk border, once the stomping-ground of Thomas Gainsborough, who recorded its every mood, and virtually unchanged to this day. Over the river, on an imposing iron bridge, the remains of a lock on the old Stour Valley Navigation can be seen through willow woods to the left. This ran from the quays of Sudbury (now sensitively restored with its Georgian warehouses converted into a theatre) to the sea at Harwich, transporting agricultural produce and the famous Ballingdon bricks (used in the construction of London's Liverpool Street Station). Effectively killed off by the railway, it nevertheless lingered on until the mid 1920s and there are long-term plans afoot to reopen it to leisure traffic.

Journey's End
And so to Sudbury, through the outskirts flanked by willow woods and water-meadows round a sharp curve and into the remains of the station. The original terminus was on the site of the present hypermarket at the far end of the old goods yard. The line to Cambridge, now a footpath past the buffer stops, necessitated a sharp curve and a new through station to avoid the town centre. Until recently, the original buildings and platform survived intact, but now all is swept away. The present station houses Sudbury Town Museum, providing a fascinating glimpse into the town's past; and but a short walk brings us to Market Hill, site of one of the largest open-air markets in the border country, on Thursdays and Saturdays, when the town is alive with countryfolk.

An ancient town of charm and character, mixing Georgian and medieval architecture and flanked by three imposing wool churches, Sudbury is bounded on three sides by the Stour and water-meadows, common land held by the Freemen of the Borough since before the Norman Conquest.

Visit Gainsborough's house, home of Thomas, and view his work before taking a stroll through history around the town. An excellent town trail guide is available from the Library – itself converted from the imposing Corn Exchange on Market Hill.

For the more adventurous, the line onwards from Sudbury is now a country trail, ending at Rodbridge Corner, now a Country Park, but once the only level crossing in the country to be operated by a member of the Russian nobility. From here it is only a short step up the hill to the notorious Borley Church, home of one of the best documented ghosts in the country. A local bus from the bus station (turn right at the end of the station approach) will take the traveller to Melford or Lavenham, both jewels in the crown of Suffolk, one of the most underestimated counties in Britain and one for which a trip up the Stour Valley line makes a fitting start to a journey of discovery.

WITHAM–BRAINTREE

by Trevor Garrod

Doctor Beeching wanted to close this six-and-a-quarter-mile line in 1963. At that time, the service was operated by a diesel railbus seating fifty-six people.

Local users fought the closure proposal, won a reprieve and then, with remarkable support from the local council, set about promoting the service to boost patronage. Patient, steady work, including the twice-yearly distribution of publicity leaflets, brought results. A two-car diesel multiple unit, seating 126 people, was needed in place of the railbus by the mid 1960s; then, in 1972, a three-car train providing 168 seats. In 1977 the line was electrified and it now enjoys a basic hourly service by four-car multiple units to and from London's Liverpool Street Station, also connecting at Witham with Colchester trains. It is not known whether the good Doctor has eaten his words . . .

The electric train leaves Witham Station on a sharp curve, with a 10 mph speed restriction, but is soon accelerating swiftly on the straight single track out into open country. It hugs the north side of the valley of the tiny River Brain, across which can be seen the red-brick Faulkbourne Hall in its park.

Three miles from Witham is White Notley Station – rebuilt in 1977 to replace an old wooden structure. To the left, across the river, the village clusters round St Etheldreda's Church with its white clapper-board bell-cote, typical of Essex.

Cressing Station is vintage Great Eastern Railway and, like White Notley, is staffed by one man who also operates the crossing gates. It serves Cressing and Black Notley, two villages with much modern housing, on opposite sides of the valley, which now narrows as we see Braintree ahead, dominated by the spire of St Michael's Church.

Passing a golf-course on the left and a factory on the right with UKF Fertilisers freight sidings, we swing round a curve into Braintree Station. Only one platform is now used, the remains of the other disappearing under brambles. Adjacent are car parks whose area has expanded as the service has grown in popularity.

This railway reached Braintree in 1848, and was extended to Bishop's Stortford in 1869. By 1966, the western section had closed completely. The ancient town of Braintree developed silk and engineering industries and, nowadays, also attracts London commuters. A short walk from the station is the busy market-place, a good range of shops, eating- and drinking-places, and the Old Town Hall which now contains an Arts Centre and a display of local history. Close by is the bus station, whose services include a half-hourly one to Halstead and a less frequent one to Great Bardfield through the showpiece village of Finchingfield.

SOME MAJOR CITIES AND TOWNS

NORWICH by Louis Hipperson

In the fifth and sixth centuries, Anglo-Saxon invaders travelled across the North Sea and up to the head of a long inlet that vanished during the Norman period. Here, in open country, they settled in a group of 'wics' (villages) on either side of the River Wensum. The most northerly of the villages, Northwic, gave its name to the town that was formed through their fusion by 1004 at the latest. During the Late Saxon period, this town grew as a market centre, serving the prosperous agricultural area of East Norfolk, then the most densely populated part of Britain.

At the time of the Norman Conquest, Norwich was one of the largest towns in England. A royal castle was erected shortly after 1066, although the stone keep – drastically restored in 1834 – was not built until about 1160. The town's importance at this time was reflected in the removal of a bishop's see from Thetford to Norwich in 1094. Herbert de Losinga, the first Bishop of Norwich, began the building of the cathedral two years later. This was completed in the twelfth century and has the second highest cathedral spire in England (315 feet).

The Middle Ages were, in general, a period of great prosperity for Norwich, which maintained its position as one of the leading towns in the country. Its wealth was based on foreign trade carried on through its port and the multiplicity of crafts practised in the city. By the end of the fourteenth century, it was the chief centre of the worsted industry.

Despite varying fortunes in the Tudor and Early Stuart periods – marked by plagues, times of trade recession, fire, the upheaval caused by the Reformation – tax returns suggest that Norwich was probably the largest provincial town in England in 1662.

However, the city had no swift-flowing streams to provide water-power and lacked easy access to the essential raw materials of the Industrial Revolution. This caused a severe decline in its worsted industry although this did not finally die out until near the end of the nineteenth century. In 1800 Norwich was the third city in England, but by 1861 its population was exceeded by that of many Midland and Northern manufacturing towns.

Throughout the 1800s, new industries were established in Norwich, such as the manufacture of boots and shoes and the production of a wide range of food and drink. Existing industries of printing and bookbinding, banking and insurance were expanded. The last has developed world-wide connections. In the present century engineering, chemical technology, and clothing have become important. Since the Second World War, Her Majesty's Stationery Office has moved its headquarters to the city.

Nowadays, visitors by rail to Norwich can reach the centre by catching a bus outside the station. They will find that Norwich is still a thriving provincial capital, fully conscious of its glorious past, but nevertheless in the forefront of modern development. Its present population is about 120,000 with some 60,000 in the extensive outer suburbs beyond the present city boundaries. Norwich has a vast hinterland, embracing practically all Norfolk and much of North Suffolk. This explains why it has considerably more shops than many places of similar size. The shops range from departmental stores to places serving widespread specialist requirements. Bookshops – new and second-hand – abound.

The most striking witness to Norwich's importance and wealth in the medieval period lies in the ancient parish churches within the walled central area. Originally there were more than fifty. The thirty-two that remain are mostly in the

Perpendicular style and their number is not exceeded by that in any other city in Europe north of the Alps. Ruins remain of two others and a round tower is the only relic of St Benedict's. St Julian's, a Saxon church with a round tower, was partly destroyed by bombs during the last war, but has since been rebuilt.

Among other buildings of interest are the large Roman Catholic Cathedral of St John the Baptist (1894–1910); the fifteenth-century flint-faced Guildhall; and the twentieth-century brick and stone City Hall (note the Swedish influence).

The last two buildings overlook the Market Place, occupied by the stalls of the open-air provision and general goods market, one of the biggest in the country.

Norwich has a rich cultural life. The castle houses a museum and art galleries. The latter contain works of the Norwich School of Painters, the only local school of artists in England and the only one to take its name from a specific place. The city has four other museums, a large central library (with an excellent local studies department), four theatres (including the world-famous Maddermarket, as well as a puppet theatre in a disused church and an open-air theatre in the castle grounds), and many halls used for concerts and lectures. Norwich also contains the University of East Anglia, founded in 1963, and two public schools.

Other outstanding aspects of this fascinating city include many open spaces, especially parks and gardens. A First Division football team plays at Carrow Road and Minor Counties' cricket is played at the Lakenham ground. And who has not heard of the Norwich terrier and the Norwich canary?

More detailed information on Norwich is available at the Tourist Information Office in Tombland, near the Cathedral.

CAMBRIDGE by Geoffrey Roper

The national – indeed international – fame of Cambridge rests on its university and colleges, but for the city itself they have not always been an unmixed blessing. It was they, for instance, who insisted on the elegantly arcaded railway station being built (in 1845) more than a mile from the city centre. Nevertheless, it is the architectural splendours of the colleges which the rail-borne visitor comes chiefly to see, and so he or she must take the bus (frequent service from outside the station), or join the throngs of cyclists for which Cambridge is renowned.

From the centre, the historic colleges and university buildings are all within easy walking distance. A preliminary visit to the Tourist Information Centre in Wheeler Street, behind the Guildhall, can provide not only answers to general or specific queries, but also maps, guide-books, and leaflets, and, if required, conducted tours. Overnight accommodation may also be booked there.

The earliest settlement of Cambridge, in Roman times, was on the other side of the River Cam, to the north-west, in the area of the castle (now just a grassy mound in the grounds of the Shire Hall). This was followed by an Anglo-Saxon village which gradually spread southwards across the river. By the twelfth century, the present centre and the basic layout of the town was established, with its two main arteries converging at the Norman round church in Bridge Street, and the Market Place lying between them a little further to the south. In 1201 the first charter was granted to what was by then a thriving market town, and later in the thirteenth century the university came into being. The oldest college is Peterhouse, founded in 1280, and there are fifteen other colleges of the medieval and Tudor periods. All have buildings of great architectural and historical interest, ranging from the famous cathedral-like chapel of King's to the remarkable Pepys Library (complete with all the books and bookcases of the famous seventeenth-century diarist) at Magdalene. Most colleges are normally open to visitors during the daytime, except in May and June (because of examinations).

Seven of these old colleges are adjacent to the river, and the area to their rear, with lawns, willow trees, gardens, and little bridges, known as the 'Backs', has been described as 'the most perfect man-made view in England'. In the summer, punts may be hired to enjoy this view to the best effect.

The university itself, although historically less important than the colleges, has interesting medieval and later buildings, notably the group known as the 'Old Schools', with the eighteenth-century Senate House, opposite the magnificent University Church of Great St Mary (whose tower offers a good view over the roof-tops of the town). Nor must the important and sometimes controversial nineteenth- and twentieth-century architecture of both university and colleges be ignored.

A walk round the city will also reveal many interesting non-university buildings, old and new: a number of fine medieval (and neo-medieval) churches, the massive High Victorian Corn Exchange opposite the Tourist Information Centre, and the splendid Edwardian building of Foster's (now Lloyds) Bank, on the corner of Sidney Street and Hobson's Street, are just a few worth mentioning. The exploring visitor will also quickly become aware of the extensive green open spaces and commons which are one of the pleasanter features of Cambridge.

The attractive and historic villages of Trumpington, Grantchester (famous for its association with Rupert Brooke), Fen Ditton, Coton, and Histon are within easy reach. The last-named still has a railway and station building intact, on the Cambridge to St Ives freight branch, which many residents and visitors would like to see reopened for passengers.

Back in the city, it remains to mention the museums and art galleries, including the world-famous Fitzwilliam Museum in Trumpington Street, the Cambridge and County Folk Museum in Castle Street and a number of specialised scientific and archaeological museums maintained by the university departments: for full details and opening times, consult the booklet *A Brief Guide to Twenty Museums in Cambridgeshire*, obtainable at the Tourist Information Centre.

Cambridge is an important centre, with three old-established department stores, a flourishing daily market, many specialised small shops and one of the country's largest bookshops (Heffer's in Trinity Street). All in all, Cambridge offers so much to see and do, that a day trip can only whet the appetite for a more extended visit.

IPSWICH by Alan Cocker

Probably the main claim to fame of modern Ipswich is its football team (the ground is only five minutes' walk from the station), but this, and the apparent absence of glorious relics, hides a distinguished past.

Recent evidence suggests that Ipswich could be the oldest Saxon town; its port with over 1,000 years of history, was the most important in Anglo-Saxon times. It received its charter in 1200 and Thomas Wolsey, Henry VIII's Chancellor, was born here. The town has two buildings of obvious antiquity, Christchurch Mansion, now a delightful museum (admission free), and the Ancient House. To learn about the less obvious parts of the town's history it is worth joining a guided tour or buying a 'Town Trail' booklet, both available from the Tourist Information Office at the Town Hall.

Ipswich today is very much a modern town existing for its twentieth-century inhabitants. The town has a considerable range of industries, many based on agriculture and engineering and an expanding port at the head of the Orwell Estuary. Its leisure attractions include the new Crown Pools, the varied and fine-quality productions of the Wolsey Theatre, and the Corn Exchange which houses the reasonably priced Ipswich Film Theatre among many things. Live shows are often presented at the Gaumont. These amenities are in the town centre, a bus ride or twenty minutes' walk from the station. The views from the Orwell Bridge are a new attraction and can be appreciated on foot or by bus.

Ipswich is no museum piece like some places but the visitor may understand why its residents find much to be proud of in it.

COLCHESTER by Lewis Buckingham

Situated on the River Colne, fifty-two miles by rail from London, Colchester is Britain's oldest recorded town.

The main North Station, about one mile from the town centre, is connected to it by frequent buses and also by hourly local trains on weekdays to the conveniently situated St Botolph's Station.

'Camulodunum', as Colchester was known in ancient times, has a history stretching back long before the Roman invasion in AD 43. The first Roman city was founded here and, although destroyed by Queen Boadicea in AD 61, rose again to become a walled city and the most important Roman centre in Britain. Parts of the wall still stand, including the ruined Balkerne Gateway.

The eleventh-century Norman castle, built on the foundations of a Roman temple, has the largest keep built in Europe, and is now a museum in an attractive park.

Today's Colchester is a thriving town of 76,000 people with a busy port. There are many fine stores, supermarkets, and a new precinct catering for the discerning shopper. There are four museums: Hollytree (Customs and Antiquities), Holy Trinity (Social History), All Saints (Natural History), as well as the castle, and the Minories Art Gallery. Together with the medieval churches, a modern sports centre, and a Dutch Quarter where the Flemish weavers originally settled, these buildings provide a pleasing mixture of ancient and modern.

The Town Hall with its fine clock-tower was completed in 1902, and it is there in the Moot Hall that the annual Oyster Feast is held. The 'natives' (oysters) have been famous since Roman times. The Town Hall also houses the Tourist Information Office.

Standing in the shadow of 'Jumbo' (the Victorian water-tower), the Mercury Theatre provides entertainment throughout the year.

During the summer months, a sightseeing tour by open-top bus is available. Dedham, in the heart of Constable country, is also easily reached by bus as are Colchester Zoo and many attractive villages, while the coast is easily accessible by rail and bus.

LOWESTOFT by Trevor Garrod

Lowestoft's growth in the nineteenth century from a large fishing village to a sizeable town (population now over 60,000) was due mainly to the railway and its associated docks. The station is thus well sited for the fish dock (not open to the public; but guided tours are available to organised groups) and the shopping centre (recently pedestrianised).

Just to the south of the railway is Lake Lothing – the inlet which cuts the town into two and serves as the commercial harbour. Immediately to the south of the bascule bridge is the remarkable building of the Royal Norfolk and Suffolk Yacht Club, the yacht basin, and then two miles of sandy beach with two piers and a good range of public gardens and amusements, backed by solid and stately Victorian terraces built in the town's heyday as a fashionable 'watering-place'. On this lively stretch of beach, during the season, will be found Punch and Judy, trampolines, and life-guards; while seafront attractions include putting-greens, boating-lake, crazy golf, and tennis – all within a few minutes' walk of the station.

A mile to the north of the modern centre is the old High Street, leading to the lighthouse, Belle Vue Park (naval memorial), and Sparrow's Nest (maritime museum). On the northern edge of the town are Pleasurewood Hills Leisure Park and a nudist beach.

Details of town buses and where to catch them are displayed at the railway station and there is a town map in Station Square. For nearby Oulton Broad there are also buses – but many visitors and local people prefer the five-minute train journey to one of its two stations.

SOME STATELY HOMES
BY PUBLIC TRANSPORT

by Lorna Knight

Several of East Anglia's stately homes can be reached by public transport, and many are within easy cycling distance of a railhead. All the stations mentioned here are served by trains on which bicycles are carried free of charge.

I personally visited the following during the summer of 1984:

FELBRIGG HALL
Three miles from Cromer Station, one and a half miles from Roughton Road Halt. National Trust. Ordnance Survey Sheet 133, 20N 39E. (Telephone West Runton 444.)

A seventeenth-century house with eighteenth-century furniture and an outstanding library. Walled garden; parkland with lake. Generally open afternoons, April–October. Lunches and teas in old kitchen.

Felbrigg Hall is a pleasant walking or cycling distance along a minor road out of Cromer. A taxi may be hired at Crisp's, (telephone 512564), near Cromer Bus Station.

For full details of current opening times of the hall, write or telephone the Administrator, Felbrigg Hall, Felbrigg, Norwich NR11 8PR.

SANDRINGHAM HOUSE
The Norfolk home of the Royal Family is open on most days from late April to late September. For details telephone the Estate Office, King's Lynn 2675.

There are frequent local buses from King's Lynn Bus Station (five minutes from the railway station); but I travelled on the Coastliner (Service 780) limited stop bus service which operates four days a week in July and August, from Great Yarmouth to King's Lynn, and calls at Sheringham Station Approach. The Coastliner bus, in 1984, was not practicable from King's Lynn on weekdays nor from Great Yarmouth or Sheringham on Sundays.

HOLKHAM HALL
Some two miles west of Wells-next-the-Sea, Holkham Hall is an impressive eighteenth-century house owned by the Earl of Leicester and set in a large park. It is open three to four days a week, June–September and light refreshments are available.

I travelled by train to Sheringham, where I caught the Norfolk Coastliner bus for just under an hour's journey westwards, alighting at the Victoria Hotel, Holkham. The hall is about one mile's walk from the bus stop.

Lunch is available in Holkham village at the Ancient House and at the Victoria Hotel. A very sustaining meal can be obtained at the Chinese Take-Away, next to Sheringham Station, to eat on the train on the way home. Remember to request a spoon!

It is also possible to reach Holkham from King's Lynn by bus, either on the Coastliner or on Sunday (Service 411).

For current details of opening times and entry charges at the Hall, telephone Fakenham 710227.

BLICKLING HALL

This seventeenth-century red-brick house is situated one and a half miles north-west of Aylsham (Ordnance Survey Sheet 133, 18N 28E). It is a National Trust property, generally open to visitors April–October. For current details, telephone Aylsham 733084 or write to the Administrator, Blickling Hall, Blickling, Norwich NR11 6NF.

Attractions of the hall include a textile conservation workshop, a gallery with a Jacobean plaster ceiling, parkland and a lake. Teas, morning coffee, and lunches are usually available; and lunchtime refreshments can also be obtained at the adjacent Buckingham Arms.

The nearest station is North Walsham, eight miles cycling distance along quiet roads to the east. Aylsham has an hourly bus service from Norwich, and a two-hourly bus service from Cromer and Sheringham. One can walk from Aylsham to Blickling, along a fairly busy road; or a taxi is available (telephone 734185).

Six further suggestions are:

ANGLESEY ABBEY, Lode, Cambridge. A National Trust property with a 100-acre garden, the house dating from about 1600 (telephone Cambridge 811200).

Lode is six miles north-east of Cambridge and is served by hourly buses from Cambridge and Newmarket. (A change may be necessary at Burwell on some journeys.)

PECKOVER HOUSE, North Brink, Wisbech (telephone 583463). A town house built about 1722, with a Victorian garden. National Trust. March Station is nine and a half miles away and there is a direct bus link to Wisbech; while the town is also served by the Rail Link Coach described earlier in this book.

ICKWORTH, Horringer, Bury St Edmunds (telephone Horringer 270). This National Trust house was built 1794–1830 and contains Regency and late-eighteenth-century furniture. It was a walled garden and park. The nearest station is Bury St Edmunds, three miles away.

WIMPOLE HALL, Arrington, Royston, Herts. (telephone Cambridge 207257). This eighteenth-century mansion, with work by Gibbs, Flitcroft, and Soane, is now a National Trust property. It stands eight miles south-west of Cambridge and its nearest stations are Royston (six miles) or Shepreth (five miles – no Sunday service).

A bus service from Cambridge to Biggleswade serves Wimpole Hall.

BEESTON HALL: An eighteenth-century house two and a half miles north-east of Wroxham, open on Sundays, Bank Holidays, and Fridays from Easter to mid September (telephone Horning 630776).

HOUGHTON HALL (telephone East Rudham 569). An eighteenth-century house, home of the Marquis of Cholmondeley, Grand Chamberlain of England and a descendant of Sir Robert Walpole. It is a good destination for the more energetic cyclists, being fourteen miles east of King's Lynn in the direction of Fakenham, and can be reached by minor roads. It is open Sundays, Thursdays, and Bank Holidays from Easter to September.

FOR FURTHER READING AND REFERENCE

BOOKS

The East Anglia Tourist Board (14 Museum Street, Ipswich IP1 1HT) publishes a cheap but comprehensive annual guide that gives opening times of places to visit. The Board also produces information sheets and leaflets – many of them free.

Among the series that include a volume for each of the counties covered by this book, the 'Shell Guides' (published by Faber) and the 'Little Guides' (Methuen) (of pocket size) are particularly recommended. 'Red Guides' (Ward, Lock) are available for certain parts of the region, mainly coastal areas. 'The Buildings of England' series, edited by Nikolaus Pevsner (Penguin) (two volumes for Norfolk, one each for the other counties) are essential reference material for anyone interested in architectural history. Full details of all these works, including whether they are in print and current prices, and advice on other suitable guide-books, should be obtainable from any public library.

As to books of substance on the general history of East Anglian railways, regrettably almost none are in print. However, the following is worth consulting:

Swinger, Peter W. *East Anglia.* David & Charles, 1983. (Railway History in Pictures') £6·50. Despite the series title, this book has an excellent introduction, packed with information, and generous text between illustrations.

Worthwhile books *out-of-print* include:

Allen, Cecil J. *The Great Eastern Railway*, 5th rev. ed. Ian Allen, 1968. Gordon, D. I. *A regional history of the railways of Great Britain*, vol. 5: *The eastern counties*, 2nd ed. David & Charles, 1977.

Joby R. S. *East Anglia.* David & Charles, 1977. ('Forgotten Railways' series.) Deals with dismantled lines.

Simmons, Jack. *The railways of Britain: an historical introduction*, 2nd ed. Macmillan, 1968. Contents include 'A complete analysis of the railway system in a single county, Suffolk.'

Lincolnshire by Rail – a similar rail guide-book to this one is being published by the Lincolnshire Branch of the Railway Development Society, covering the area north of Peterborough. It will be available in April 1985 at £1·80 from many bookshops or direct from Mr J. Saunders, Stockwell Gate, Whaplode, Spalding PE12 6UE.

MAPS

Ordnance Survey publish maps of various scales, each series suited for particular purposes. For further details write to Information and Public Enquiries, Ordnance Survey, Romsey Road, Maybush, Southampton SO9 4DH.

Bartholomew: The following maps in the National map series (5/8 inch to 1 mile) embrace the region: 16 – Essex; 20 – Cambridgeshire (except Fens); 21 – Suffolk; 25 – Fenland; 26 – Norfolk. Further particulars from John Bartholomew & Sons, Ltd, Duncan Street, Edinburgh EH9 1TA.

TOWN STREET PLANS

G. I. Barnett & Son Ltd, Rippleside Commercial Estate, Ripple Road, Barking, Essex IG11 0SB (many East Anglian towns).

Colour Maps International, 145 Crostwick Lane, Spixworth, Norwich NR10 3NG (a few towns in Norfolk and Suffolk).

Mr Wilfrid George, 43 Linden Road, Aldeburgh, Suffolk IP15 5JH (drawer and publisher). (Certain towns in Norfolk, Suffolk, and North Essex; footpath maps in rural areas also; some plans are the most up to date available.)

TIMETABLES AND LEAFLETS

British Rail publish a Passenger Timetable for the whole country, of over 1,200 pages. This is issued in May each year (usually with one or two supplements during the following twelve months) and can be bought at staffed stations and at booksellers.

A free timetable booklet is published for London–East Anglia train services which covers most lines mentioned in this book. A separate free timetable booklet is available for services from King's Cross to Cambridge and Peterborough.

Pocket-sized timetable leaflets are also obtainable, free, for individual lines, as are leaflets on taking bicycles by train.

Details of bus services are generally published in free leaflets by Eastern Counties Omnibus Company (for Norfolk and Suffolk) and its associated company Cambus for Cambridgeshire. Bus stations and local libraries can supply these.

Suffolk County Council's footpath maps and guides can be obtained from libraries or from the County Planning Department, St Edmund House, Rope Walk, Ipswich, Suffolk.

WHAT IS THE RAILWAY
DEVELOPMENT SOCIETY?

The Railway Development Society is a national, voluntary, independent body, formed in 1978 by the amalgamation of the Railway Invigoration Society and the Railway Development Association, both of which were founded in the early 1950s.

Its aims are the retention, improvement, and greater usage of rail transport, for both passengers and freight.

The East Anglian Branch of the Society covers the region described in this book; while the Society has a dozen other branches plus some area groups, covering the rest of Great Britain, and maintains contact with similar-minded bodies in this country and abroad.

Associated with the Society are many local rail-users' groups throughout the country, including groups covering nearly all the lines in this book. Together with these local groups, the Society aims to provide a nation-wide voice for rail-users. We publish books and papers, hold meetings and exhibitions, sometimes run special trains, and generally endeavour to put the case for rail to politicians, civil servants, commerce and industry, and the public at large; as well as feeding users' comments and suggestions to British Rail management and unions.

Membership is open to all who are in general agreement with the aims of the Society, and subscriptions (as at April 1985) are:

Standard rate:	£6
Reduced rate (for pensioners, full-time students):	£3
Families:	£5 (plus £1 for each member of household)

Subscriptions may be sent to the East Anglian Branch Membership Secretary, Mr L. G. Hipperson, 16 Marsh View, Beccles, Suffolk NR34 9RT.

All other inquiries about the Society and its associated groups should be sent to the East Anglian Branch Secretary, Mr T. J. Garrod, 15 Clapham Road, Lowestoft, Suffolk NR32 1RQ. Mr Garrod would also welcome any comments or suggestions for future editions of *East Anglia by Rail*.

Ancient House, Ipswich.